11/30/21

For WesLee,
Enjoy!
Loren Spiotta-DiMare

Curling Up with Cats

True Stories of Feline Rescue and Adoptions

Edited by
Loren Spiotta-DiMare

J. Pace Publications
PO BOX 301 • CALIFON • NJ 07830

D1733489

Dedication

*For all cat lovers as well as Murphy and Dickens,
two wonderful cat brothers who inspired me
to produce this book.*

Introduction

I've loved animals for as long as I can remember and greatly enjoy writing non-fiction books about them for both adults and children. My first reference book, *Macaws* was published by TFH Publications in 1979. It was followed by *Siamese Cats* in 1983.

Whenever possible, I like to meet my subjects. All these many years later, I remember ringing the doorbell of a Siamese cat breeder. When she opened the door, I was also greeted by nine friendly and inquisitive cats.

We conducted the interview in the breeder's kitchen with all of her friendly felines milling around us. One in particular climbed up on my shoulder and sat there while his person and I discussed Siamese. Needless to say, the visit gave me great insight into the behavior and personalities of the breed!

Over the years, I've had 22 books published. Most have been about dogs and horses. Although I do have two children's books entitled, *Hannah's House Rabbit* and *Broke Leg Bear.*

During book signings, I'm often asked if I have a cat book. Based on those inquiries, and a friend's adoption of Dickens and Murphy, I decided to produce *Curling Up with Cats: True Stories of Feline Rescue and Adoptions.*

Dickens and Murphy, two beautiful and personable orange cat brothers were abandoned in their first home. I was mortified when I heard the story. Luckily my friend, Mary Lou discovered the Boys at St. Hubert's Giralda Animal Welfare Center and adopted them. They are two of the most affectionate and fun cats I have ever met. (Their story appears on page 103.)

I've included a story about my Uncle Roland who rescued a wonderful cat decades ago. But all of the other stories were contributed by cat owners who rescued or adopted their feline friends.

Cat lovers are passionate about their pets as you will see as you read the heartfelt stories within these pages.

Enjoy!

Loren Spiotta-DiMare

Editor and Publisher

"I have studied many philosophers and many cats. The wisdom of cats is infinitely superior."

—William Shakespeare

Contents

Arthur

By Mary Piekarski

As America prepared to celebrate Independence Day, Hurricane Arthur swept through New Jersey, leaving behind an orphaned kitten in the woods near our community pool. This poor baby was no more than six weeks old, soaked to the bone, and starving. Thanks to the keen ears of some lifeguards who heard the mewling, he was swooped up from the underbrush and brought over to our house. Tiny and bedraggled, he was given a bath and food straightaway and as much loving as a frightened creature can handle! Having eaten with gusto, he appeared much happier and seemed to delight in the attention of the five young women who rescued him. All wanted desperately to be his mother, of course, but only one family had a strong connection to a rescue group, Cattitude, Inc., who agreed to sponsor this baby and provide the medical attention he needed. We agreed to foster him in hopes of finding him a home. How could we say no? We were already in love!

In honor of the conditions of his discovery, we named him Arthur. Arthur began life here in my daughter's room (she was one of the rescuers) while he was tested for disease and inoculated, as we already had a cat and dog we needed to protect. Once he was given a clean bill of health, his world expanded, and he enjoyed supervised explorations of the rest of the house. It wasn't long before my daughter officially adopted him; our home became his forever home, and he was a true member of our family. All of our friends had already placed bets that this kitten wouldn't be leaving our house! The other rescuers came to visit often until they had to return to college. Since that first sighting, Arthur has not lacked for any kind of comfort, love, food, toys, bedding, even playmates!

Since Arthur's adoption, our feline family has grown! Unfortunately, our first cat, an adoptee from a shelter I volunteer with, is a "grumpy cat" and doesn't want to be friends with anyone except for his humans (and on his terms). In fact, I had adopted him fearing no one else would, and it broke my heart to see him so unhappy in the shelter. This first cat, Burnett, embodies the aloofness that some people consider to be a cat's way. However, he can also be loving and never fails to make us laugh. I wouldn't want Burnett any other way. Thankfully, Arthur with his endearing mannerisms counteracts Burnett's attitude and has proven how sweet and social cats can be. Our Labrador wanted so badly to be best friends with him, and these two did become buddies, but there was a big size discrepancy. Fortunately, along came Bonneville, another adoptee from the shelter who, like Burnett, was in danger of never being adopted because of his shyness (or in Burnett's case, bad attitude). Extremely skittish and scared, Bonneville soon warmed up to Arthur, and they became the best of friends! It was wonderful to see the turnaround in Bonneville, and young Arthur was happy to have a playmate closer to his size!

It is fair to say that Arthur's sweet personality paved the way for other cats in our house. Seeing how cats can get along and enjoying their interactions, we agreed to foster and then adopt two more homeless kittens who play well with everyone (except Burnett, of course) and love our Lab. So this one rescued, scared, abandoned kitten who captured our hearts has been the impetus for the rescue of three others as well. That's quite a feat for such a tiny creature! Plus, the joy and fun we have all had (feline, canine, and human) while watching the antics between us all have been a blessing that we would not have experienced had the pitiful voice in the woods not been heard that day. Thank you, lifeguards. Thank you, Cattitude, Inc. And most of all, thank you, Arthur, for letting us love you and for opening up your heart to the others who came after you.

Bodhi's Tale

By Cheryl Hammel

Cats, like life, are unpredictable. They sit serenely one moment only to dart off in a mad dash without warning or reason; travel great distances to reunite with us long after we think they might even exist, let alone remember us; and fall from impossible heights only to land on their feet before nonchalantly continuing on their way. And, of course, they steal (and break) our hearts by coming into (and departing from) our lives.

It is that break, that inconsolable injury we suffer when they depart, that feels impervious to any healing. Anyone who has ever loved and lost a cat knows what it's like. Toys on the floor once vigorously played with are now sadly still. That certain spot by the window, on the back of the couch, or near us in bed, is now painfully vacant. Anywhere and everywhere we are faced with bittersweet reminders of our beloved cat—and our loss.

There are a variety of ways people deal with this loss. Some will rush out immediately and adopt a new cat. Others will swear to never have another cat as long as they live, saying the hurt is too much to bear. Then there are those who acknowledge the pain and loss are unavoidable and inevitable, so they work to accept it. However, that acceptance is reluctant, because along with it comes a sense there is nothing that can ever ease the pain. These are the ones who truly believe there will never be a day that goes by without sensing that empty hole in their heart, the people who present a brave face and go about their daily lives while wishing and waiting for the day and its charade to end; this I know because I was one of them.

Anyone who ever met our male tabby, Teemo, knew him to be a truly unique and amazing cat. Friendly to everyone, he was the purr-fect combination of love, curiosity, and energy wrapped up in the softest of orange fur. Teemo literally never hurt a fly; he lived to play and cuddle. He also wielded an unstoppable resilience, which no doubt allowed him to bounce back with vigor regardless of how many emergent surgeries he underwent for urinary blockages, stones, or crystals (even after having his bladder rupture from being catheterized!).

It is only fitting then that such an incredible cat departed in an incredible way. To be fair, I have loved and lost several cats, and they each will forever hold their own unique place in my heart. But the night Teemo left, more than my heart was broken. He had been valiantly fighting multiple ailments for some time. The time came, though, when his little body could battle no more. Obviously frustrated with the limitations his failing body was imposing on his irrepressible spirit, Teemo lashed out and latched on…to me! In his exasperation and discomfort, he bit and BROKE my finger! This from an almost nineteen-year-old, weak, ill, little old man of a cat who weighed barely seven pounds! Yes, one last incredible chapter in the life of our remarkable Teemo who left scars on my heart and my hand one cold Saturday night in November.

For months after he left, I was in pain. My heart hurt. My finger hurt. If someone had told me this was how it would happen before that night, I never would have believed them. Teemo? Bite someone, let alone me? NO WAY. Our other two cats—two girls—tried as cats do to draw near and offer comfort. Though their warmth and their presence were precious and genuine, there is no substituting one cat for another. And so my sorrow continued.

Life continued, as the saying goes. After all, there's a job to get to, dishes to wash, and laundry to fold. Life went on, the chores went on, and so did I—reluctantly. But there wasn't a single day that went by that I didn't feel an unrelenting emptiness inside of my heart. The drudgery of daily life and agony of Teemo's awful departure made it harder to get up every day—harder than I would dare admit.

Several months later, I learned a friend of mine had been diagnosed with breast cancer and was undergoing a double mastectomy. My heart sank. She, like Teemo, was always upbeat, energetic, and fun. It seemed like just another horribly sad thing that shouldn't be happening. When I went to see her in the hospital, it was clear that although her body had been compromised, her spirit was as strong as ever. She made it quite clear she had no regrets and no doubts; she had a life to live and a daughter to raise. I admired her strength and resolve. Despite this, I still felt sad seeing her lying in that hospital bed, a force to be reckoned with but restrained by the limits of her own body—much like Teemo.

Seeing her that way was a reminder that I was overdue for a screening. Like many women, scheduling a mammography isn't especially high on my list of favorite things to do. In fairness, since Teemo left I'd had several of my own health matters to deal with: the finger he'd bitten and broken had gotten infected and had to be lanced, I went to physical therapy for a few months to regain mobility after it healed, and I'd undergone another surgery for an unrelated issue as well. Nevertheless, if there was anything good to come from seeing my friend in the hospital that day, it was the motivation to get my overdue screening scheduled and done—soon! I hated going but I'd hate to be in a hospital bed even more. Besides, I'd been through my fair share of bad stuff lately so naturally everything would be just fine.

Try then if you can to imagine my dismay and disbelief at being told during the screening about an irregularity of concern that warranted a biopsy, right away.

This was it, way more than I could even begin to comprehend. First, Teemo, then my finger, the infection, my surgery, my friend and now…a biopsy? I'm just here for a regularly scheduled checkup, just another ordinary screening, no big deal, just another day. What do you mean an "irregularity"? A biopsy?! But you don't understand: I can barely have blood drawn without fainting, and you're telling me you want to perform a needle biopsy on my breast?

I thought of my friend and her resolve but knew that would never—could never—be me.

I thought of my job and how frustrating and disappointing it was; how it seemed no matter how hard I worked, I wasn't getting anywhere.

I thought of my Teemo and how much my heart still ached, how I could so easily cry although months had gone by.

I thought of my life in general and acknowledged that I'd basically been going through the motions, living without being alive, smiling without being happy, pretending to be engaged when all I really wanted was to disengage, to just go away and be left alone. It would be comparatively easy, too; after all, I have no booming career, no great love life, and no children to worry about.

And it was then I determined I would not be like her; I would not go through and endure what my friend so bravely faced without question. If the biopsy proved what the doctor feared it might, so be it — I will live out whatever time I have without telling anyone and without treatment or surgery. I will just let it run its course, and when it's done, I will be free. It was only this notion, this secret possibility of freedom and release, that gave me any hope.

Until I met Bodhi.

My ex knew how much losing Teemo had hurt. After all, he felt it, too. He loved Teemo as much, if not more, than I did. He also knew (purely by accident and timing) of my doctor's concerns and my impending biopsy. He then decided without telling me to look for and find a new orange male cat that he hoped and believed would give me hope, comfort, a reason to smile. One day he sent me a picture of this wide-eyed orange kitten that appeared to be sitting on furniture in our very living room! When I promptly asked with shock who is that and where is that, he responded with the rescue society's contact information and a simple message that read: If you want him, he's yours.

All of the pain and sadness and fear I'd been (poorly) managing in recent months subsided. I immediately contacted the society and applied to adopt him. I'd never applied to adopt an animal before, so the whole notion was quite foreign. Even crazier was the thought that maybe he was already adopted—or maybe they would deny my application! But life, in its unpredictable way, had already sealed our destiny.

Within hours I received a call congratulating me on the approval of our application and letting me know that Bodhi was mine if I wanted him. He would be available to pick up the next day at the pet store about forty-five minutes away. The next day, I asked, why not tonight, like right now? The voice on the phone replied with a chuckle that unfortunately no, he's about two hours away but he's definitely mine and tomorrow would be here before I knew it.

And for the first time in months I spent a sleepless night full of anticipation and excitement instead of tears.

When I saw him at PetSmart it was love at first sight! The second I saw this ridiculously adorable kitten I forgot about everything else. I hugged him close to me and held him against my heart. The ache and fear that had been haunting me fell away. I forgot about all the annoyances of work, the disappointment of life, and most of all, the anxiety of my impending biopsy. All I wanted to do was be near this beautiful little life, this wonderfully warm puffball of fur and innocence, this amazing miracle my ex and God had brought into my life. This three-month-old orange male kitten who'd been abandoned by his birth mother and left alone when his sisters were adopted had, like me, suffered some of life's harder, unanticipated developments. Yet it was life and its unpredictable ways that now brought us together in this place and this moment where our hearts were immediately and forever bonded.

Much like I would have never believed anyone who told me Teemo's last day on this earth would unfold the way it did, I also would have never believed I would meet and adopt my ridiculously adorable Bodhi. What's more, I certainly never believed there could ever come a day that the wounds Teemo left in my heart when he bit my finger and left this earth would ever stop aching. I was proven wrong on both fronts.

Neither people nor cats can be substituted for one another; each has their own special place and meaning in our lives, and rightfully so. I believe that if you are capable of providing a safe, healthy, loving home for an animal, then you should do it. I know that there comes a day when that relationship will end and, more often than not, that day is painful and not easily forgotten. But if the price I pay for knowing I've provided a safe, healthy, loving home to an animal is the heart-break I suffer on the day they cross over, so be it. What's more, I now know that heartbreak CAN be eased—all it takes is time, faith, ac-ceptance of life's unpredictable path, and the bright curious eyes of a ridiculously adorable kitten!

Boris

By Antoinette Fabre

---

oris, our first rescue kitty, came to us in January of 2000 just
a few months after we lost our Cocker Spaniel, Scarlett, in
September of 1999 at thirteen years of age. Boris was eight to ten
weeks old, and our oldest son Damien found the little guy at our
front door when we lived in Orange County, California. The house
was empty after the loss of Scarlett so when Damien found Boris,
my husband, Rocky, said we could bring him in the house as he was
way too young to be out on his own…who would let a little guy
outside with no way to get home, no food or water, too young to
fend for himself? So Boris slept in the bathroom overnight. We fed
him some tuna and got some dirt for a litter box and a cushion for
him to sleep on until the next morning when I could go to the pet
supply to get him kitty supplies. We didn't know if Boris was male
or female as he was so young and would have to wait until his vet
appointment. I went to the pet supply store in the morning and got
him food, a litter box, food and water dishes, treats, toys, a crate, a
lavender collar, ID tag, and his first of three scratching posts—bird
bath style. We gave him October 18, 1999, for his birth date, Sweethearts Day, as he touched our hearts from the minute we saw this
little black kitten at the door!

When I came home I made his first vet appointment and called to get him pet insurance, as Scarlett had pet insurance; our pets are part of the family so they had health insurance like us humans. When we took Boris to his first vet appointment, we were told he was a male kitty. Now, both my husband and I are animal people, but we both only had dogs. Boris was our first kitty! Out of the gate we taught him to walk on a leash and roll over and ride in a chest pack. He also had his own car seat!

Boris settled in very fast and was very spoiled. He had all the attention at the house being the only furry kid. We got him all his shots and had him neutered. Boris was the king of the house. He had such an awesome personality; he was very loving and got along with any other animal he was around as long as the animal was cat-friendly. Boris was the only child until our Brittany puppy, Lexi, came to us in July of 2000 at eight weeks old; when she got home, Boris was the perfect big brother to Lexi. She was, after all, the first dog he was really around being only 9 months old, and they were both fine together.

He ran on a flexi leash just like a dog when we took him and Lexi to the schoolyard to run. He walked on a leash with her when we would go to the hardware store or for a walk at the beach! We also rescued a little baby sparrow we named, Tweety who fell from the nest, and we bottle-fed him until his feathers came in and he got old enough to eat worms and seed. Boris would sit with Tweety and just hang out, Tweety would fly in the house and land on the cat scratching post to hang out, and never did Boris ever try to hurt Tweety.

There was so much Boris did for the family. He even helped raise our next rescue kitten, Natasha. She was just two pounds and four weeks old when we got her in 2002. She came with her certificate of adoption from her foster parents, Henry and Elizabeth, also the pet supply store customers and a kitty rescue family. Natasha was so very small and young that she started to bite at Boris a few times until he said enough and bit her back—well, she understood at that point biting was not a good thing. We started to Field Trail with Lexi, a pointing dog sport, and with that we would travel while Lexi was competing, and we brought everyone with us. So at a hunting dog sporting event with lots of other dogs, we were with our cats; Boris, who walks on a leash and has never been around a dog who was not cat-friendly in his life, and the group that we competed with and against were blown away seeing Boris walking on a leash and calling the coyotes in at night while talking in the trailer window so anyone could hear him talking.

So the story of Boris being a big brother continues, as shortly after Natasha came to our home. I was at a good friend's son's high school graduation party. When it was time to leave late in the evening there were four cats—a mother and her three kittens, two girls and one boy. I used sandwich meat from the party sandwiches to get the kittens and mother cat who were strays come to me, so I was able to bring them home. I got all four of the them home; we got mom and brother and one sister to the animal rescue in Orange County, California, and we kept the other female and named her Chloe. She was going to be another youngster Boris was going to deal with as a big brother. Chloe was also small and young—just a few months old, perhaps a month or so younger than Natasha, so Boris now had two young female kittens who just moved into his house! Boris was great to both of the girls; they both loved Boris, and with him being older, he looked out for them and made sure to keep them in check.

We then got our male Brittany, Steele, in 2003; he was four months old. Steele never saw a cat before but he was drawn to Boris, and again Boris rose to the occasion as he did in the past to make the newest and youngest addition to our family feel safe and welcomed. Boris would be sleeping on a pet bed, and Steele would lay down with his head across Boris's back. The contrast of Boris being an all-black cat and Steele being orange and white, but primarily white, made for great pictures. Boris was such a good sport, as Steele would chew on him a little here and there while playing with Boris. But no one was ever hurt, as everyone has always been expected to get along with each other as a family.

In 2004 I ended up bringing home a young chick a friend had but thought it was a quail; the school her daughter went to had done the egg hatching program so she had the bird at her apartment and had asked me if I wanted the quail, who was really a chicken named Lola. I said yes as she couldn't keep the bird in her apartment as it was growing. So I brought Lola the chicken—who was then small and used to being handled—home to the house that now has two hunting bird dogs and three cats. Who knows what Boris was thinking, let alone the rest of the gang. Really? A chick in Huntington Beach, California, living with three cats and two dogs? Boris was fine with Lola. She would sleep on top of her cage with any of the cats with no problem. Even when Lola became Spike, crowing and acting tough, Boris was still patient and had no issues with Spike!

So as time went on, Boris was just such an easygoing, loving cat. He was good with all the rest of the family, our two boys and all of our furry kids. A few years later in 2008, when Boris was nine years old, we moved to Inland Empire Riverside County. While I was doing dog and cat food demos at a feed store in Norco, California, I brought home a ten-pound, three-month-old potbelly pig who we named Kirby. So Boris again was a big brother to Kirby, the baby potbelly piggy!

Kirby slept in a cat crate until he outgrew that and moved to a dog crate. During the day Kirby would sleep with Boris as the girls, Natasha and Chloe, slept together. Boris was always the one to make the new kid feel at home.

Then in 2011 we got another Brittany puppy, a little brown and white female named P.J. She was a little older when we brought her home at seven months old. She did have a cat at her last home, but she was not as close to that cat as she was to Boris once she was home with us. So Boris, now twelve years old, was again forgiving and put up with P.J. as she was a little rowdy pup compared to Lexi and Steele. Now being the youngest of the furry kids, she tested Boris and is no lady as she likes to play rough, but Boris held his own with P.J. just fine.

Time goes so fast. It is truly just a blink, and now Boris is coming up on seventeen years old on October 18, Sweethearts Day. Well, our Boris was diagnosed with cardiomyopathy and congestive heart failure. He lost weight and started to get fluid around his lungs and abdominal area, so we had it drained. We put him on a medication regimen as there was no surgery to help give us more time with our Boris. He had a few gray hairs but for being almost seventeen he was still our handsome boy. Bless his big heart, he took all the treatments like a champ. He didn't like most of what we had to do to help him; oral medication was never easy for us to get him to take, but we made it work as best we could. He did fine for a while, and we were hopeful to celebrate his seventeenth birthday, and we did! We were, of course, in denial, hoping we would have another few years with him. He loved the car rides but as time went on, it was harder, and the trips to the vet would tire him out. We knew he was not going to get better but hoped we would have him here with us for Thanksgiving and Christmas.

The last week and a half it was clear that it was getting close to the time for him to say goodbye to us and cross over the rainbow bridge to join our Lexi, who we lost in 2013, and Scarlett, who Boris came after. His last week he used an oxygen mask Rocky made from a clear plastic cup and clear tubing, and Boris knew it helped him breathe. He could see through it so he was good with the mask, and it helped him breathe easier so he didn't fight it. His last week, Steele slept next to him on the bed just like when Steele was a puppy, and Chloe did the same. They knew he was sick so they laid close to him to keep him company. His last day with us was November 15, and he was at home when he passed away. It was the shortest seventeen years ever, and we were so blessed to have had that little black kitten come to our front door and into our lives and hearts. Our sweet little boy Boris, we love and miss you, and you made a difference. He is with us every day, and he rescued us as much as we rescued him.

Butters to the Rescue

By Rena Davis

A re black cats bad luck? I have two enormous parlor panthers, Butters and Dewey, and I always thought that because they were in my life, I'd acquired some kind of magical immunity to black cats crossing my path and to bad luck in general.

We adopted Butters and Dewey as kittens from our vet, who does pro bono work with strays. My Traditional Siamese had just passed away. She was a stray who adopted us when we lived in Virginia, and in honor of her life, I wanted to adopt another homeless cat. While we had two big dogs to help ease the pain of this terrible loss, I really missed having a feline presence in the house. We were looking to adopt a kitten, since a new feline would need to acclimate to our dog-rich environment. When we visited the veterinary clinic, a vet tech handed us two little black kittens, one to my husband and one to me. The vet tech explained that they were brothers, had always been together, and which one did we want? It would have been too sad to separate them (well played, vet tech, well played…), so we took them both. We figured that cats are pretty independent and low maintenance compared to dogs, so we probably wouldn't be able to tell the difference between caring for one cat or two cats.

In no time at all, Butters and Dewey grew into two fine, almost identical cats. You can only tell them apart by behavior. Dewey always looks a little worried and is more skittish; Butters is very outgoing and at ease in any situation. As long as they aren't moving quickly, I can tell them apart at a glance. They were a wonderful addition to our family, and I've never regretted having two cats in the house. Both keep their claws to themselves and are gentle with both humans and dogs.

At the time of this story, I was working as a director at a pharmaceutical company and life was a hot, hectic mess with quite a bit of travel. Right after returning from a meeting halfway across the country, my company sent me off again to attend an executive boot camp at Harvard Business School. I repacked my bags and once again left my furry tribe in the care of my very capable husband. The training sessions were absolutely exhausting, and I was looking forward to getting home and staying there for a while. When I returned to my family, Butters was at first his normal, friendly self, but out of nowhere, he suddenly scratched me very badly across the chest while I was carrying him. There had been no provocation, and I could not figure out why he had done this. It was completely out of character for him, so I queried my husband to see if anything had happened while I was gone. Maybe Butters was ill and this led to an unexpected change in my normally sweet and loving cat. My husband had nothing to report that could account for this strange behavior, so I ended up just shrugging it off as one of those things and decided to keep an eye on Butters. Maybe he was sick and the symptoms were subtle, so my husband hadn't picked up on them.

After a few days, I felt a lump where he had scratched me. Oh great, I thought, I have a swollen lymph node and cat scratch fever. Thanks so much, Butters! A friend of mine had gotten very sick and developed golf ball-sized swellings in his armpit as a result of leaving this infection undiagnosed and untreated. I thought the symptoms were the same and, knowing that I'd get really sick if I didn't do something about it, I cursed my luck and made an appointment with the doctor. Dealing with the infection was going to be inconvenient. My mind clicked off the points of how it was going to disrupt my schedule and it was going to make it harder for me to make my timelines and I had better think ahead and delegate some stuff and…and…and. The list went on and on, because as always, I was hugely busy. I truly resented being forced to make time to visit my primary care physician before this thing progressed and really took me out of action. When I went to the appointment, tapping my foot and checking my watch, I fully expected her to make the diagnosis and then to send me on my way to pick up some antibiotics before returning to work in time for the next meeting. But life is full of surprises. Instead of walking out of there with a simple prescription, my doctor immediately contacted a surgical oncologist. Her suspicion of breast cancer was quickly confirmed by a series of diagnostic tests that culminated in a biopsy. The final diagnosis after a bilateral mastectomy was two tumors, one of which was invasive, just one tiny step away from metastasizing.

Maybe it was coincidence, but I like to believe that Butters somehow diagnosed the cancer and saved my life. Butters has never scratched me since, so who knows? However this came to be, I count myself as being extremely lucky because I adopted black cats.

Caleb, Our Rescue Cat

By Laurie Farnkopf

Caleb showed up at our door one rainy August night nine years ago. My husband and I heard a noise and thought it was a cat; we heard it again and realized it was a kitten. After much coaxing with food, we were able to grab him and bring him inside. My exact words were: "I am calling the humane society in the morning. We have too many other cats." My husband said, "But this one NEEDS us."

A few months later we found out just how much Caleb needed us. After many, many vet visits, tests, medications, and several thousand dollars later, we found out that Caleb has Wolff-Parkinson-White. This disease causes the heart to race continually and could possibly kill him. He would lay on the floor, lifeless, his little heart racing out of control. We were actually asked if we wanted to euthanize him. I said, "Are you kidding? He is only a one-year-old cat, so that is not an option." Thankfully, a few years later, we found a veterinary heart specialist who finally found the right combination of medications that has stopped the attacks.

We are well over $10,000.00 now. He takes three different medications; one of them has to be compounded, made just for him, but he is worth every penny. He is the most loving, beautiful cat, and I can't imagine our lives without him. We did save him from a shelter and probably saved his life. It was very difficult to actually figure out what was wrong with him. Endless vet visits, tests, medications. We had to track his heart rate daily. Through the veterinary heart specialist, we found a vet surgeon in Ohio that agreed to try to operate on his heart but warned us that the instruments she would be using are not fit for his tiny little heart. They have had success with larger breed dogs, but not cats. So we decided not to do that, which was a very hard decision, since at that time, the medications were not keeping his heart rate under control.

It was pretty crazy, but thankfully, he has not had an issue for a few years now! We do worry, he is on a lot of medication, but we do truly cherish each day he is healthy.

Cat Sitter Needed

By Joanne Masar

"Hi, we are Kiddie 1 and Kiddie 2. We are two sweet brothers looking for a reliable person who would like to feed us two times each day while our homeowners are away. We do not need any extra attention but would like our litter box changed once a day."

These two homeless scoundrels would come around begging for food. We found them to be neighborhood pests and had no use for these two vagabonds. We would do everything to ignore them!

Then the worst nightmare, Hurricane Sandy! Living on the water, our neighborhood was a disaster area. We were not able to go back to our home for a few days after the storm. To our amazement, one day there they were, these two cats with their noses pressed up to our door. They both looked so beat up and scared. I can only imagine what they went through during the storm! Being survivors, they must have been smart enough to get into one of the boats and ride it through!

We felt sorry for them but still did not encourage them to stay around or come into the house. As neighbors started to return to the area I went door to door to see if I could find out who actually owned these cats! I finally found out who they belonged to. After taking them back to their owner a number of times, they would always show up the very next day at our door!

OH NO! A snow storm and the bold one was at the door wanting to come in! OH NO! What do I do? Feeling guilty, I still stood firm and refused to let him come in out of cold. I could not give in and let this bug-infested creature inside, fearing he would never leave! After he reluctantly sauntered away, I thought 'Ok, he will find a safe, warm place.' But no, I had to look outside and there he was across the street on the neighbor's porch barely visible in the icy snow! I could not stand it any longer. I opened the door and called, "Kiddie, Kiddie!" He barely was able to lift his head up but he heard me and came running! Thus the name Kiddie was sealed!

Since then we have been through many trials and tribulations with getting locked in a neighbor's shed, getting trapped under the dock, getting beat up by a dog, and the list goes on. When Kiddie 2 became sick, I said enough already and took both Kiddies to the vet and had them completely checked out, debugged, and given all the required vaccinations.

Now Kiddie 1 and Kiddie 2 have become indoor cats with a new home, their own beds (plus ours), lots of toys, always fed, and special treats. They are very sweet and so funny, making me laugh every day with their antics. We are all blessed to have each other. Just a note to those who think you are not cat-friendly: Just try it, you will not be sorry!

David and Daisy

By David Donchek

M y name is David, and I'm from Boston. This is the story of how I met my beloved cat, Daisy.

On November 10, 2001, I became sober after decades of drug and alcohol abuse. I owe my sobriety to an inpatient program at a local VA Hospital. During my stay I was introduced to the ID clinic and the wonderful staff there. At this time, I met DeDe, a nurse at the clinic. Not only was she my healthcare provider, but she became a good friend, too. I was about to start my new life of sobriety in my first apartment, and DeDe and the clinic staff helped me out with new dishes and other staples that would get me started. By the way, they did this for everyone, not just me. I spoke about how my life would be complete if I had a cat. One block away from the VA was the animal hospital, which was also an adoption center.

One day the secretary from the clinic, Paula, offered to take me over to the adoption center to look at cats and then she would drive me home. A friend I met in my alcohol support group gave me a carrying case to have when I did get a cat to take home. I walked up and down the aisles looking at the large selection of beautiful cats. Every variety from Siamese and Persian to your plain old domestic cat was there, and in every color of the rainbow. It was overwhelming to see all those cats who needed a home.

All of a sudden I spotted a cat and on the cage said "Whitney, two years old." I assumed she was named after Whitney Houston. When I approached her cage, she came from the back to the front to greet me. None of the other cats did that. They seemed to be indifferent to me, probably thinking just another human passing through. Whitney rubbed her face against the cage, and I stuck my hand close for her to smell me. Paula said with so many beautiful cats, why don't I look some more. I did, but kept coming back to Whitney. She was a Tortie, and she was gorgeous. She seemed to talk to me with her big beautiful eyes. They were telling me to take her home. My mind was made up, but I wasn't crazy about that name. From that moment on Whitney became Daisy.

When I went to the clerk at the adoption center, I was told that if I wanted her I would have to wait since Daisy had an abscessed tooth that would have to come out. I could come back in two days and get her. I believe Daisy didn't have much time left; I might have been her last hope to get a home or they would have put her down. They weren't going to do anything about that abscess had she not been adopted. We went to the desk to do the paperwork, and Paula told me that DeDe would be paying the $100 adoption fee. She knew how much I wanted a cat and that my funds were very low. I was filled with so much joy for having found a new friend, but to realize that I had friends who cared so much about me to want to give me this gesture of love was overwhelming. I returned two days later to pick up Daisy, who was now missing a front canine tooth. She looked so funny, and it made her even more lovable.

Daisy and I started our lives together. She became my absolute best friend. As the years passed, my sobriety became stronger and so did our bond. Daisy seemed to know whenever I was down and would come sit on my lap and rub her head in my hand. Daisy was a little strange in the fact she didn't purr like other cats I've had in the past. I could feel a vibration coming from deep within but never actually heard her. Nevertheless, I always knew when she was content and happy. She was also a kneader. She loved sitting on my belly and just kneading, and I'd break out into laughter as sometimes it would tickle. My belly would go up and down from laughing, and she'd never move, just bouncing along like a Coney Island ride. I'd look at her and ask, "Are you baking a cake?" and she would just keep kneading, looking me straight in the eye while doing so.

In 2008 I lost my mother. I made the trip to New Jersey where she was in hospice. My sister, Marilyn, and I were in the room when she passed. She suffered for her last year, and it was almost a blessing to see her so peaceful. I spent a week in New Jersey, and Daisy remained back in Boston. A good friend who has a dog walking service in Boston would visit Daisy every day, making sure her box was clean and she had fresh water and food. She would sit and play with her for about a half hour and leave me notes on how she was doing. When I returned home she instinctively knew I was sad. She greeted me with lots of rubs and quite a bit of chatter. I forgot to mention, Daisy was a talker. Sometimes it seemed she never shut up. At times it almost seemed we were having a conversation in this strange language that only we knew. I always felt Daisy had some Siamese in her blood because of the amount of yapping she did. The loss of my mother left a strange, unfamiliar gap in my life. Those daily phone calls and frequent trips to visit with her would be no more. I guess we learn to adjust.

Through the years I had several surgeries. In 2010 I had my left hip replaced. It was a breeze, and the relief from pain was almost instantaneous. I recovered at home and Daisy was my nursemaid. I had to keep moving because my little girl still had her needs. It was good in a sense because it helped speed my recovery. I loved when Daisy would sleep with me. She would be at my head on my right side. I always found it funny and amazing at the same time that as many times I would get up during the night, she would never move. I'd come back from my many nightly trips to the bathroom and there she would be, like she never heard a thing. She was aware of everything. Nothing got past her. One night we were sitting on the recliner, and she was sound asleep in my lap. All of a sudden she lifted her head and made a mad dash into my bedroom. I followed her there only to find she was whacking around a tiny spider. Till this day I don't know how she heard it. It was like the time when I first moved into my current apartment. She would sit in front of the oven just staring underneath. This went on for days. Finally, I called my landlord and said I haven't seen anything, but I think I have a mouse. The maintenance man came up and moved the oven only to find some mouse droppings in the open area where the electrical wires came in for the oven. He stuffed it up with some wire mesh and the problem was solved. A few weeks later Daisy was again sitting right back there, and without hesitation I called the maintenance man to come back. Sure enough, they chewed through the wire mesh and were back. This time he put this foam that expands and becomes hard as a rock. I've never had this problem again.

Daisy was getting on in her years, as I was. She developed a problem with digestion, and the vet told me to mix some pumpkin in with her food. It seemed to help with her pooping situation, but she continued to vomit almost daily. She'd have an episode, then would be fine like nothing happened. My trips to Angell Memorial were becoming more frequent. The doctor and her assistant were wonderful with my Daisy. We had some tests done, and my worst fears would come true. Daisy had pancreatitis. The doctor said she could go on for a while and might have an episode every now and then. She prescribed a certain food that needed to be ordered through the hospital's pharmacy. We went home; we would just have to see where things would go.

Nothing much was really different for months. There were good days and some not so good. Finally, after a week of things not being so good for Daisy, I brought her back to the doctor. More tests were done, and it didn't look good. On top of the pancreatitis getting worse, other problems were starting to develop. They wanted to keep her for a couple of days and run more tests. At that moment I made the decision that I could not put my little girl through any more torture. I felt I was only keeping her alive for my selfishness. She was a good friend, and I couldn't see her suffer anymore. So on April 22, 2015, I would put Daisy out of her misery. The doctor brought me into a special room and soon brought Daisy into the room with me. They had her wrapped in a towel and an IV drip with fluids attached.

They left me alone with Daisy. I sat with her for over an hour. I held her weak body close to mine. We just stared into each other's eyes. I reflected on the fourteen years we had together. Counting the two when I got her, Daisy was sixteen years old. I was so glad I was able to provide a good home for her. Through good times and bad she was there with her unconditional love. I rang for the doctor. I held her tight as the syringe with that lethal dose was administered. Within seconds I felt the life of this wonderful living creature drain out of her body. As I write this on the page, tears are running down my face like they did at that moment. They took Daisy out of my arms, and I left through a side door crying like a baby. I was in my car driving home crying, and I suddenly felt a dampness in my lap. Daisy had peed on me as she died. I started to laugh, thinking she left me with a final gift.

Needless to say, when I walked through the door to my apartment the loneliness sank in. In the next few days I started to get rid of everything belonging to Daisy, from her litter box to food and toys. I donated some of the things to Angell Memorial. My friends and family were so nice during my grieving time, but nothing could get me out of my depression. I didn't think I would want another cat in my life. Did I have the energy or the strength to take on the responsibility? That answer would soon come in the way of a phone call from my good friend Lorna.

She said a friend had a pair of eleven-month-old Siamese mix cats that needed a home. One was given to her next-door neighbor, and they were looking for a home for her sister. I said I would take a look without making any promises. I went over to look; I looked into her blue eyes and knew I had a new friend. I named her Lucy, and May 30, 2015, a little more than a month after I lost Daisy, we went home to start what has become another wonderful friendship. I'm glad I was used to a cat that talked a lot, because Lucy is a real chatterbox. I compare Lucy to Daisy sometimes, but she has her own personality, and it's quite different. As a single man who has lived by myself all my adult life, people may not understand the bond you develop with a pet. My cat is my child. If anyone ever stood by my door and listened to the conversations that I've had, they might think I'm crazy, but those are the conversations that have kept me sober and kept me from going crazy.

Gabby, the Rescue Tabby

By Kim Andresen

My name is Kim Andresen, and I recently adopted a four-year-old rescue cat. I am in my senior year at college, living away from home. Growing up I always had pets around. This rescue story started because I missed the companionship of our current family cat, so I decided I wanted to foster a cat. I chose a no kill rescue shelter not far from my apartment, which took any cat or dog that was in need of help. One of the first things the shelter asked was if pets were allowed in my rental apartment I knew my lease said no pets, but I decided to take a chance and ask the landlord for permission to foster a cat. Luck was with me that day because by some miracle he said yes, and the fostering was on. I was so excited when I told the shelter that I had gotten the go-ahead from my landlord. As excited as they were to hear that I got the go-ahead, they needed to confirm this with my landlord and said they would get back to me soon. I waited patiently to hear when I could go pick up a cat. It took three days but finally they called and said I was approved to foster a cat so I could come down to the shelter to pick out the cat I wanted to foster.

I rushed to the shelter and asked the owner which cats had been there the longest. She gave me a list of five cats and said, "Any of these will work." I went up to each cat and opened each cage. Although they all were great cats, they just were not the right cat for me. I continued looking at the other cats in the shelter and came across this small, gray cat that looked pretty beat up and was only about five pounds. She was sitting in the corner with a half missing ear, a squinting eye, and holding her left leg kind of funny. I looked at her name tag and asked the owner if this small cat had been there long. She replied that the little gray cat had been at the shelter for six months, but she implied she didn't put the little gray cat on the list because she did not think the cat would get adopted. She told me, "But if you would like to foster her, she could use the love." I let this little gray cat out, and she barely looked at me. She wasn't very playful, or particularly affectionate, but she was calm, and I found her to be very cute, so I decided to take her home.

As I was packing the cat up, the shelter gave me a little history about the cat. She came from a hoarding home in West New York with eighty-six other cats and five dogs. She had been locked in a dog crate with five other cats for what they thought was three years and was never allowed out. She lived in the cage with no cat litter, and the hoarder dumped food into the cage in order to feed all the cats. The shelter also mentioned that the little gray cat had never been in a house on her own so she had no idea how the cat would react in an apartment and that the cat was not that friendly with the other cats in the shelter.

When I got home, I let the cat out of the cage, and she immediately lit up. She did not show any fear; even with her bum leg she was running around everywhere and exploring everything. After a few minutes of running around and exploring she came and sat on my lap, purring loudly as if to say thank you. That was the moment I knew this cat was something special. She limps, she had one and a half ears, and her one eye squints all the time, but it gave her character, and I knew she appreciated everything.

For the next two months I tried desperately to get this cat adopted. I tried every way I knew to get the word out about the cat. She was perfect in every way in my eyes but there was no luck. She was affectionate, playful, and an all-around well-behaved cat, but the first thing everyone saw was that she was already four years old and her imperfections. After trying very hard to get her adopted, I decided that maybe the reason she wasn't getting adopted was because she was meant for me. This was an obstacle because I am graduating college this year and have no clue where I will be next year. This makes it hard to know if I will go somewhere that accepts cats or if I have to move home.

Our family cat at home has been alone in the house for eleven years, and I did not know how she would react to another cat. I decided to bring the small gray cat to my parents' home to see how she would do and try to convince my parents that this small gray cat was meant for me. I decided that if it was meant to be, the two cats would get along. I brought the little gray cat home, and she got along with my other cat after some days of introductions and minor hissing. After a few days at home my parents agreed she was something special, and we all agreed to keep her. I was so excited that I immediately called the shelter and informed them she had found her forever home, and it was with me. They were ecstatic!

I named this little gray tabby Gabby since she is so vocal, and we have been together for three months. There are some health problems like the bad leg and the eye that I am mindful of every day, but it doesn't stop her. In addition to her medical issues, she shows signs of mental scarring that I am learning to accommodate. She is very afraid of quick movements and anything that is lifted over her head. I am slowly showing her that people can be trusted, and she is showing me how resilient she can be. She has put on some weight, her coat has become shiny, and her eyes are always bright now. I am so glad I did not overlook this little cat when I was choosing a foster cat as she's changed my life. We have a long road to recovery ahead of us, but it doesn't matter because we are doing it together.

The news article and video about the hoarding house she was rescued from can be found at this link: http://hudsoncountyview.com/86-cats-5-dogs-rescued-from-west-new-york-animal-hoarders/ She can be seen in the video at the 0:20 second mark in the cage with the other cats. She is the one in the front, and her left ear is missing half of it.

Goldie and the Three Stooges

By Kathy Miele

On the bank of the Oceanport Creek stood an old farmhouse. There were several Adirondack chairs its huge wraparound porch. That's where you could usually find Goldie, the gray and brown tabby cat, curled up and napping during the hottest part of the day.

Goldie had been watching over this waterfront home for several years, making sure it stayed clear of mice and voles, so the family that lived in the farmhouse didn't have to worry about anything getting in. Goldie loved her job, but she was getting older, and she began spending more and more time curled up in her Adirondack chair.

One day the family car pulled into the driveway. Goldie lifted her head to greet them as they walked over and placed a cardboard box in front of her. Looking over the edge Goldie saw three orange tabby kittens. Three brothers named Larry, Moe, and Curly looking up at her.

Goldie wasn't particularly pleased; she had enough to do at the farmhouse. The last thing she wanted to do was train these three boys in the art of pest control. But each morning someone from the family would bring the cardboard box out to the porch and Goldie would try teaching them. She'd run through the reeds, flushing out any pests, hoping the three boys would join her in the hunt. They watched her from the porch, but they didn't join in. Goldie wasn't sure what to do with them. They seemed content to stay on the porch.

Finally, Larry was the first to explore the property. Goldie watched as he made his way down to the river, through the gate, and onto the dock. He gazed over the edge of the dock and watched the schools of minnows swim by, while the crabs scurried on the muddy bottom. Larry's eyes tracked the minnows, and Goldie watched from the front yard as Larry quickly dipped his paw into the water and flipped a small minnow onto the dock behind him. Larry stared at the small minnow, flipping and jumping on the boards of the dock. He finally scooped it up in his mouth, walked back down the dock and through the gate, and placed the minnow on the ground in front of Goldie.

Not sure what to do, Goldie decided to do what she'd done with all the gifts she'd caught on the property. She showed Larry where to drop the minnow: at the back door on the porch. When the owners came out they laughed and shrieked. Goldie saw how happy they were to get the fish. So, as a reward, she took Larry over to the Adirondack chair and groomed him.

The next day, when the owner came out with the box of kittens, Goldie was anxiously waiting at the back door. Larry hopped out of the box first and went to the dock to fish. Goldie felt she could leave him alone so she could work with one of the other kittens. She watched as Moe slowly climbed out of the box and began to venture around the yard. Goldie watched as he tracked the birds in the trees, but quickly lost interest. That was a good thing because Goldie knew the owners never liked getting birds as gifts.

Goldie watched as a vole scurried through the reeds along the water's edge, but Moe still wasn't interested. Just then, a small breeze came by, and a few brown leaves tumbled across the lawn. Moe was ready for the chase! Batting and tumbling along with the leaves, Moe finally captured one between his paws. He proudly looked Goldie's way, took the leaf in his mouth, and pranced over, placing it in front of her.

Goldie had no idea if the owners would want a leaf. She'd never brought them one. But she showed Moe to the back door and had him place it there. When the owners came out and saw Moe with the leaf under his paw they burst out laughing. Goldie saw how pleased they seemed and, as a reward, brought Moe over to the Adirondack chair and gave him a good grooming.

The next morning as the box of kittens came out of the house, Goldie once again was excited to see what the last little kitten would be able to hunt. Larry jumped out of the box and headed straight for the dock. Moe ran to the brambles, waiting for some stray leaves to capture. But Curly stayed in the box. Goldie peeked over the edge to see what Curly was doing. Curly looked up and gave a soft meow before slowly climbing out of the box and sat by the edge of the porch. Goldie checked on the other two kittens, then returned to Curly who by now had climbed up in the Adirondack chair, waiting for Goldie to join him. Goldie climbed up in the chair next to him, and Curly quickly began to groom her.

Goldie was caught by surprise. No one had ever groomed her before! She wasn't sure what to do. But after a few moments she finally leaned back and enjoyed her bath. When the other two kittens dropped their gifts at the back door, they, too, climbed up in the chair. Wrapping themselves around Goldie, she could hear their soft purring. She'd had no idea how much she needed these three stooges.

Just the Right Spot

By Robert Grayson

Spot first started exploring my backyard when he was very young. He couldn't have been more than six months old. This adorable black-and-white tuxedo kitten probably found me because he saw an older, all-white male cat coming over to the house for food. Named Snowball by my wife, the white cat had been showing up every day for both breakfast and dinner for months.

Initially, Spot just watched as Snowball dug into his morning and evening meals. But Spot wasn't a shy fellow. He ambled over one day when I put out Snowball's food and literally tried to muscle his way into the dining area.

To keep things civil, I placed two bowls of food on the ground, and it wasn't long before this tuxedo kitty became a regular. I named him Spot because he had a marble-sized black spot on the back of each of his white paws.

Snowball always wanted more than just food. He enjoyed hanging around me, getting petted, and being a part of my life. Spot, on the other hand, would simply eat and run.

After feeding both cats for a while, it became evident that neither one of them had a home. While Snowball would inch his way closer to the garage from time to time, Spot didn't seem to want to have anything to do with domesticated life—no petting, no hanging around, no rubbing up against my leg.

I often wondered if Spot understood he could come to me for shelter during a violent rainstorm, a blizzard, or a heavy windstorm. Snowball knew he could count on me for help in a pinch. But Spot was rough around the edges and seemed determined to make it on his own. He was wary of people, even though I had been feeding him religiously for months. He'd gobble up his bowl of food and vanish until the next mealtime.

Spot was now appearing for breakfast and dinner, growing bigger and stronger every day. You could see he was going to be a hunk once he was full grown. Sometimes he exchanged a hiss or two with Snowball, and then off he went. His fur was coarse and disheveled; he had some scratches—he was obviously a feral cat.

Despite his indifference toward Snowball, Spot established an endearing friendship with a rather unusual companion. I'm not quite sure when the two became friends. Spot had been visiting my home for months before he brought his friend along with him, a young, befuddled-looking Dachshund.

Pokey, as the Dachshund was called, managed to wiggle his way under his owner's fence several times a week and get out of his front yard. He'd wait for Spot to come along and walk with him to my house. Occasionally, as I saw them approach, I would hear a few soft barks from Pokey and Spot responding with two or three meows. I don't want to imply they were having a conversation, but I did have to wonder about it sometimes. Regardless of the language barrier, they seemed to understand each other perfectly.

They made quite a pair. Spot strutted with confidence and determination. Pokey, by contrast, waddled alongside him, uncertain as to their destination but trying to keep up.

Pokey relied on Spot for these forays through the neighborhood. Without Spot, Pokey could never make his way home.

The lovable Dachshund had an atrocious sense of direction. And though he lived in a home that was just a block away from mine, he simply could never find his way back. Sometimes Pokey would head for home without Spot by his side. The young pup would take a few steps, stand in the middle of my driveway, and turn around and around as if he were trying to get his bearings. The quizzical look on Pokey's face in these moments of utter confusion was priceless. He seemed to be saying, "I know my house is around here someplace. Gimme a minute. It'll come to me. There it is. Nope. There it is. Naw. Eh! I don't know where it is. I'm lost! Lost!" Spot would quickly come to his aid, taking the lead and walking him home.

Curious about their travels, I followed them several times and watched as Spot led the diminutive brown dog right up to his front door. Then Spot would turn around and return to my property, having given his canine friend another good day out on the town.

Both Snowball and Spot were getting known in the neighborhood. While some communities might not be thrilled with a feral cat or two, Snowball and Spot were providing a valuable service. Mice abounded in basements and garages in my neck of the woods before these two intrepid felines showed up. After they were around for a few months, that mouse problem was becoming a thing of the past. So they easily won over the hearts and minds of the folks who lived here.

Snowball and Spot loved their wooded, suburban surroundings, and managed to keep out of each other's way. But dangers were lurking out there, and Spot stumbled onto one of them.

On a dark, chilly December evening, Spot didn't show up for dinner. Snowball arrived, but no Spot. I looked around for him for a while, but he was nowhere to be found. So I fed Snowball, left some food out for Spot, and went inside.

At about 10 p.m. that night, a good four hours after Snowball and Spot usually ate their evening meal, there was a loud banging at my front door. I opened the door and, to my amazement, there stood Spot with his left paw raised. He was much more boisterous than usual, meowing rapidly and loudly, and I could see that his left paw was swollen. He readily came into the house, limping as he did.

Once inside, Spot was surprisingly well-behaved, showing none of the standoffishness that was his trademark outdoors. I'd always heard that wild animals would lash out when they were sick or injured. But not Spot. He was very congenial, even relieved that I was willing to help him.

41

I examined his paw and cleaned it off, but saw no bleeding, no reason for the swelling. Yet after a while, Spot's paw swelled up to the size of a handball.

We brought him to the vet and there, too, Spot was a real gentleman. He let the vet examine him without a fight, and after several tests it was concluded that Spot must have stuck his paw into a burrow of some sort and disturbed another animal's peaceful rest. The startled subterranean dweller apparently bit Spot's paw, causing an infection, and that explained his vastly oversized appendage.

Other than his injury, Spot passed all his tests with flying colors. He was a healthy outdoor cat with no trace of disease. Even though he had scratches and other signs of wear and tear, he was in good shape overall.

But the infection in his paw was extremely serious; without surgery, Spot might die. So the energetic tuxedo cat was scheduled to go under the knife immediately.

As the flurry of veterinary medical attention accelerated around him, I kept waiting for Spot to respond by growling and hissing. Instead, he was a model of gracious forbearance. All the vet's assistants fell in love with him. He let everyone pet him, and hardly anyone could believe he was a feral cat, living on his own.

Yet the evidence was indisputable—he was dirty and scratched and needed a touch of home care. For his surgery, Spot got cleaned up and medicated. Following the operation, he had to wear a lampshade collar or, as it's known in the veterinary field, an E-collar, to prevent him from licking or picking at the bandaged paw. He needed several weeks of oral antibiotics and a few months of indoor rest.

I thought the task would be insurmountable, but Spot was an exceptional patient. To my surprise and amazement, he took his medicine like a trooper and adjusted to indoor life as if he had been born to it. He was even stoic about wearing the lampshade collar.

It seemed this brief encounter with the wildlife around my home persuaded him to give domestic life a try. And he liked what he saw. A few weeks later, a major snowstorm convinced Snowball to take a shot at staying inside as well. They have both remained converts to the indoor life ever since.

At times during Spot's recovery, I saw Pokey wandering around the neighborhood and took the confused but congenial canine back to his house. Months would pass after Spot was injured before Pokey finally mastered his surroundings and found his own way to and from my house on his own. Once he did, Pokey would come around to the rear of my house where he visited Spot.

The now-domesticated feline loved to sit and look out a big glass door at the rear of my house. The two buddies would greet each other through the door, but Spot never showed any interest in going outside. Living indoors, where you didn't always have to watch your back—well, for Spot, that was the life.

Fortunately, after his recovery from his injured paw, Spot never suffered any ill effects from the mishap. He claimed a nice soft cat bed he found in my house, and relaxation became a new pastime for him.

He also turned an unlikely place in my home into one of his favorite haunts. Though a burly, muscular fella by now, Spot would cram himself into a small, round, porcelain sink in a powder room in my home and comfortably sleep there for hours. I could never understand why he liked it in the sink, as opposed to some roomier location in the house he could have easily chosen. But he could snooze there in the sink better than some people could sleep in their own beds.

A short time after Spot's surgery and his embrace of domestic life, my wife and I noticed a sign in town promoting a clean streets project. It urged people to adopt a small area of each block and keep it clean. The program was called "Adopt a Spot." We were tempted to stop and leave a note on the sign: "We already have."

A Tale of Many Kitties or How I Learned to Love Cats

By Susan Moore

All my life I have been a dog person. It's not that I didn't like cats; dogs were just more appealing. I would, however, feed the stray cats that were around. About seven years ago, I noticed a tuxedo cat. I would leave him food occasionally. One day a small tricolor kitten came with him. The kitten was a friendly female.

She came around every day, coming up on the porch and even peering through the back door. I named her Brownie. Soon she allowed me and my family to touch her. As often happens, she brought some littermates, a black male kitten and another tricolor female. I still owned a dog, and Brownie delighted in teasing her.

Soon we fashioned a cat house from a plastic storage container and insulated it for warmth. Brownie and now Blackie (very original) were welcoming but the tuxedo and the other tricolor were skittish. We became very attached to Brownie, and unbeknownst to me my son was bringing her inside. I also realized the tuxedo was the patriarch of this little colony. He dominated all and mated with the females. With this revelation, the last thing I wanted was a lot of kittens so I decided to have Brownie spayed. The other tricolor, now named Preggers, was already pregnant but she didn't stay around all the time. I was sure that after Brownie's procedure she would never come back. I was wrong.

Preggers had her litter, I don't know where or what happened to them. Another tricolor female soon joined the loop. She was friendly, and my son thought she was a neighbor's cat named Kiki. We also thought she was the mother to the three cats we now had in our yard. Things started to get crazy. Kiki would run in the house, and we had a heck of a time getting her out. Then she got pregnant. Since our neighbors were neglectful, Kiki came around all the time to be fed. She had her litter elsewhere. Again, I don't know what happened to them.

Summer came and both females were pregnant again. The old tuxedo sickened and died but not before he let me pet him. I knew he was grateful for all our care. It was in his eyes. The kittens came, and I started to get very concerned. What would my neighbors think? The cats did roam in their yards. I knew I had to do something. Only two male tabbies survived from one litter, and we found homes for the others. I got Blackie fixed while Preggers was still unapproachable. Of the two male tabbies, one was friendly, named Pud, but the other, named Runty, was not. When the time came we got Pud fixed. This was helping the population problem.

My beloved dog passed away at this time, and I was heartbroken. Every day when I came home from work, Brownie would greet me.

She'd go up the stairs and roll on her back for me to pet her. It was like she knew I was sad and wanted to comfort me. It was then I began to change my view of cats, as I always thought they were aloof.

In December 2011 Brownie left the yard, and I never saw her again. We searched to no avail. Heartbroken again. Two weeks later, Preggers also disappeared. We never knew what happened to either of them.

The time had come to have Kiki spayed since she rarely left our yard. Her personality changed but all the cats get along fairly well. They all came in the house at will now except for Runty. Since all the fixed cats got shots at procedure time, I wasn't concerned about disease.

Pud disappeared suddenly and then reappeared six weeks later. A little thin, but otherwise fine. This gave us hope that Brownie might come back, but she never did. Runty was unapproachable but still around. He started bringing a friend, a pretty orange tabby who was obviously pregnant. We named her Cissy, and then when they were old enough, her two kittens, Bootsy and Patchy, starting coming with their mom. Now let me stop here to discuss the effect this was having on our lives. My husband was not happy. My kids were loving it. I was worried. What if my neighbors called animal control? I wouldn't blame them, to be honest. The colony mostly stayed in my backyard and surrounding woods but they did go on other properties. My morning routine was being taken over by tending to cats. I now had a litter box to clean daily. The hair, the smell, the fleas, and ticks! What had I gotten myself into? I researched cats and cat behavior and vowed not to get too involved. If they disappeared, I would accept that; if they became ill, no veterinarian. I spent quite a bit of money tending to sick dogs with unsatisfactory results. I would let the cats live their life their way, and let nature take its course.

Superstorm Sandy came, and though I tried to keep the cats safe, all but Kiki went outside. Our home and neighborhood were flooded badly. Kiki slept through the entire thing. We saw Bootsy, the kitten, on our fence and tried to rescue him but he ran away. Later we heard pathetic crying across the street. My son braved the storm to investigate. He found Bootsy cowering between cars covered in motor oil. He brought Bootsy in and cleaned him up, and he spent the next two days hiding under my son's bed. The morning after the storm I was sure all the cats had perished. I then heard Cissy yowling loudly, to find her kittens I presumed. Patchy, unfortunately, was lost but miraculously, all the others lived! I was amazed at their ability to survive.

Of course, Bootsy became part of our lives. He was a wonderful cat. We had him neutered and tattooed. One day he, too, went out and never came back. We searched, put up flyers, and went to shelters but nothing. We can only hope a nice person picked him up and gave him a loving home, but there was no escaping it: another broken heart.

Cissy was very shy but stayed around the colony, so she was spayed. Runty and Blackie then disappeared. Runty, well, the lack of fertile females probably drove him off. But Blackie! He was one of my originals, my connection to Brownie. I was devastated. Another futile search. About a month later Blackie came back, skinny and tired but unharmed. I was so glad. I knew I was hopelessly hooked. A few months later, Pud became ill. I broke my no vet rule and rushed him for emergency care. There was nothing they could do. We think he had a stroke. We keep his ashes.

Meanwhile, my husband was unhappy. He loved the cats but it seemed the situation could easily get out of control. He was right. A new tuxedo cat started coming around, along with another tabby and black cat, all males. I tried to chase them away, but the tuxedo persisted. He soon joined the colony, and we named him Mickey. The tabby and black cat also kept coming; only to feed, but soon these males brought females—pregnant females. This was crazy. I should not have fed them but they were all so skinny. Soon there were kittens all over the place.

Eventually, we placed the females and five kittens. My husband, who was against the entire cat thing, had his eye on a little tuxedo male. I was against this as we had recently allowed the male tabby, now named Biff, into the colony. The other black cat was not friendly but stayed around until he, too, disappeared. This was enough. Twelve cats had been a part of this colony during the four years it existed. Eight were fixed at my own expense. Two that we loved disappeared, two that we loved died. My husband agreed that a home would be found for the kitten. We had two homes lined up but both fell through so you guessed it: Felix was now ours. Unlike the others, he is not allowed out; like the others, he was fixed.

After a year of being gone, Runty came back. We still couldn't touch him. Brownie, Preggers, and Bootsy either were taken or were dead. Runty coming back convinced me of this as I know they all would have come back if they could. Sadly, Runty died several months later after getting caught in the wheel well of a truck.

We have learned to manage the colony, and there have been no new cats for two years. There are six cats in the colony. I have broken my rules about vet care. It was learned Biff was feline immunodeficient virus (FIV) + so he does see a vet, and also my Blackie was recently hospitalized for urinary problems and is now on a special diet. I treat them for parasites and get them booster shots.

I follow the trap-neuter-release philosophy. Many people disagree. The five cats do go out but due to neutering, there is no fighting. They are fed so no garbage is disrupted. The killing of birds by outdoor cats is an issue but I have many feeders in my yard, and mostly the cats stare at them. My neighbors have been great. We explained the cats are vaccinated and fixed. We have asked them to please alert us if there are problems. They actually have commended us on taking care of them and are grateful that they help keep the rodent population down.

A word about shelters and rescue groups. I have had many negative experiences. One organization said the email I sent them was too long and they didn't have time to read it. I am sure they had time to solicit donations. One well known group that often sponsors pet adoption at a big pet store wouldn't even return my calls or emails. Shelters are crowded, and even "no kill" policies are often disregarded. Not all shelters and groups are bad but researching any agency is important.

This is my tale of many kitties, but how did I learn to love cats? The plight of feral/stray cats is not their fault. To clarify, a feral is a cat that is born in the wild and is unapproachable; a stray is an abandoned cat. Irresponsible pet owners are largely to blame. These are people who will not sterilize, who move away and leave their cats to fend for themselves and think they can survive. The average life span of a feral/stray is only about six years, and they are miserable years. Cold, sick, starving years. They multiply quickly so population control is difficult.

The cats I have saved are grateful. When they snuggle up to you and give you that special look, you know they are saying thank you. They no longer worry about being shot at by air guns or having rocks thrown at them or sprayed with hoses or worse. They now have something to live for.

I would like to dedicate this story to the memory of the first dog I owned as an adult. He taught me the true meaning of pet ownership and love. His name was Bixy, and without him none of this would have been possible.

Minnie

By Herb Porter

T*he Great Depression was not just economic. Herb Porter was four years old in 1939. His four, much older brothers were working or had died. His family was poor, and although he lived in town, there were no children his age nearby. A stray kitten became his best friend. At age 75 he remembered her with this essay.*

"Canikeeper? Canikeeper?" It was just the way I excitedly ran all the words together when I asked my mother, "Can I keep her?" Sometimes I stuttered and mother couldn't understand me, but I was just overexcited, and she had to calm me down. My mother did not need another mouth to feed, no matter how small, but my pleading to keep Minnie convinced her to spoil her youngest son one more time. So she agreed to my adoption of this big-eyed, big-eared mongrel cat. She must have sensed my prevailing feelings of loneliness, rejection, and need for companionship, and she knew this abandoned, frail, starving little kitten would keep me busy. If my father said I could keep her, I knew, with her approval first, the battle was won.

What Dad would say was somewhat routine. After considerable haranguing of "another mouth to feed," his reply would be: "If your mother says it's okay, then it's okay." I had heard about a worldwide Depression and was often told starving children would be thankful for any food I didn't eat. There would never be any money for fancy store-bought cat foods, so she would have to survive on table scraps and some of my milk. Thus, Minnie and I began our five-year relationship. I still don't know why I named her Minnie. She must have liked it because she always came running to me when I called her name.

Mom and Dad had a new baby, my younger sister, to fawn over. My brother Bill had his dog and friends, but I had no one. So Minnie was more than a pet cat; I was always lonely for playmates, and until we found each other I would spend a lot of time sitting on the bottom step of our porch yearning for something to do.

It was from that very step that I saw a teen-aged kitten standing in the middle of the street. Her starved, gray, tiger-striped body was hard to see against the asphalt backdrop. I could tell she was confused as to where she was and what to do. She slowly looked in all directions, totally befuddled, obviously frightened and hungry. She was trying to decide which way to go home. I sensed I knew how she felt because I could recall being separated from my family at the carnival and the paralyzing fear that forced tears down my face. Her skinny legs did not move. Even though the Depression had all but stopped automobile traffic on the street, it still was not the place to stand or play.

I was going on five years old and not allowed to enter or cross the street without being accompanied by an adult. I was alone, so I started using gentle coaxing. My words to her and my small outstretched hand with waving fingers enticed her to my side, but she paused at each step, slowly turning her head with cautious eyes, which had shifted side to side first. Her ears, which seemed larger than her face, twitched to every distant noise.

Once she was by my foot, I was able to put my hand on her bony spine and began rubbing her ever so gently. My fingers rose and fell as they contacted her protruding ribs. She was starving. I bent over to pick her up as she arched her back against my leg. She twisted her outstretched neck and turned her head to stare up at me over her shoulder. It was love at first sight for both of us.

Up until then I had always been the needy one—wanting to be played with, fed, cuddled, protected, and loved. But now I had her and the responsibility of parenthood. I would take care of her as good parents do.

Girls had their dolls to hold, talk to, and care for; but boys did not play with dolls. Boys needed another live boy to play with, for even doing mischief was not fun alone. There were no other boys in my neighborhood, so Minnie was a blessing.

I had never seen her or any other cats in our neighborhood as there were no other pet residents on the street. Any visiting animals just passed through like hobos, wandering and unwanted. All were prodded to move on by barks from Butch, my brother's Collie/St. Bernard Mix. But Butch didn't bark at Minnie. She had won him over, too. I would see this huge dog gently hold her under his paw while she licked him. They were a true picture of "Yes, we can get along."

Minnie was a good listener and seemed to know when to purr, lick my fingers, or just rub her neck against my arms. She never ignored me, rejected me, or hurt me. I could talk about the past, the present, and the future to her. She was better than a human friend. Sometimes she would find me crying from physical punishment, hurt feelings, or overall depression. She was my psychologist, listening to the outpouring of my problems. My tears and sobbing would stop so I could tell her of my suffering. When she lay in my lap, she purred my problems away. Our conversations, though one-sided, were educational, spiritual, and uplifting.

Some days we would be together from morning to bedtime. She would play with me when my older brothers wouldn't. Sometimes it would be finger/paw boxing or kickball—where she raised her rear feet to slap a rubber ball back to me. Never a claw grabbed my clothing or skin; she would never hurt me in any way. I could have her follow me by dragging a string. Then she would lay by my side and sleep.

Occasionally, she would disappear for a day or two, but she would always come home. My mother said she wanted cat company and would return. She always did. She grew fast. Her childlike dependence on me for love, food, and protection seemed ever so short.

One notable day something outside aroused her. She was sitting on an armchair. After a rocking and swaying movement that I had never seen her do before, she turned and ran with increasing speed from one piece of furniture to the next in a giant loop around the living room. Her last leap was onto my right knee and toward the window. Without clawing me to stop, her momentum carried her through the glass pane. Its broken pieces followed her to the ground three stories below. I raced to her motionless body covered with glass chards, believing she was dead. But there she lay with eyes open in an expression of surprise. She slowly stood up, dripping glass, while my mother said,

"She just used one of her nine lives." I don't recall her using any of the other seven—only the ninth and the last.

War rationing of gasoline had ended, and traffic was picking up all over town. Street cats darted among cars without concern; not all would make it to the other side. One night I defied my parents and snuck out of the house to find her. Maybe it was fate, but I found her lifeless rigid body only feet away from where we met. I clutched her stiff body and cried profusely. I was feeling the loss of a very important loved one for the first time. She would never be there to console me, or listen to my woes, or absorb my feelings of tenderness.

I now knew the true feeling behind what my mother was saying when she uttered, "You'll miss me when I am gone." I understood the silence of the houses with the gold stars on flags that hung in the front windows.

Minnie would never greet me again, but she really was there when I needed her most. She helped me survive the hardest years of my childhood, the Depression, and war times. Now, when I see little children crying, I hope they have a Minnie, too.

My Grandcats

By Wendy Lee Klenetsky

Although both daughters married eleven weeks apart in 2013, it's my younger daughter who has given us the joys of being grandparents. Oh, before you get all weepy-eyed and curious and ask the normal questions:

(1) Is it a boy or girl? (2) What color hair does it have? (3) Who does it look like? Let me clarify things right away. You see, my baby girl has two rescue cats: hence, my "GRANDCATS."

Now while I know grandparents are supposed to love the little ones *EQUALLY*, I'm afraid that's almost *IMPOSSIBLE* in the case of those cats.

The first to arrive was Ash. He's a white cat with black markings around the eyes. Ash is what I call a "pet." He actually greets you at the door and gives you his paw. He then will sit calmly, either next to you on the couch, or by himself on any surface: top of the television, bookshelf, or the like. That's Ash, grandcat Number One.

Then there's our *OTHER* grandcat Number Two. His name is Morgan, and he's a *TERROR*. Now that may sound somewhat harsh for a grandparent to say, but once I describe him and his shenanigans, you'll understand why that name/description applies...*IN SPADES!* Let's see: Morgan, the younger, was wild and hyperactive from the moment he became a member of the family. *Hyperactive*, you ask? Well, what would *YOU* call it?

We grandparents visited one time and saw that MORGAN was sitting on the windowsill, seemingly in a peaceful dream. Then, all of a sudden, when I went to put a vase filled with (artificial) black roses (my daughter's favorites since high school) on top of the china cabinet, MORGAN jumped off the windowsill—further and faster than ANYONE in the OLYMPICS could do—jumped over the coffee table, ran into the dining room, and leaped on top of a box there. Then as I gingerly placed the vase onto the cabinet, Morgan, staring intently, practically *DARED* me to stop him from jumping up to the vase. I yelled "NO, MORGAN. GET DOWN!"

My husband, daughter, and son-in-law ran into the dining room, anxious to see what all my screaming was about. All I had to do was point to the mischief-maker. We all then had a good laugh over it.

And, of course, I couldn't leave *THIS* out:

One night, my daughter called us and related the following incident to us:

She came home from work that day. When she opened her apartment door, she found cat food *ALL OVER THE FLOOR*, leading from the kitchen through the dining room and into the living room. She was dumbfounded! *HOW* did this happen??

After she finished sweeping up the mess, in walked MORGAN. He went right over to the cat food cabinet, and, with his paws, *OPENED IT*! So, although she wasn't home to *SEE* him do it, it was obvious that the culprit was Morgan, as usual!

Oh, did I fail to mention the first time my daughter took Morgan to the vet, the doctor *ASSURED* her that once Morgan was fixed (neutered), he would be a "delightfully calm" cat. I guess MORGAN didn't read those instructions.

But everything considered, my husband and I really love both of them. After all, they are our GRANDCATS!

My Two Best Girls

By Doreen Sproviere

It was a beautiful Saturday afternoon, the sun beaming, the sky clear and blue. It was March 21, 2009. My life changed that day for the better. The spare bedroom was set up as best as could be since there was still plenty of furniture, including a double bed filling the space.

I was volunteering with a rescue organization in Westwood, New Jersey and wanted to foster. My only experience was taking care of a small colony where I worked. Feeding and socializing these feral cats were fairly easy, except in bad weather when I was battling wind, rain, snow, and bitter cold. Other than that, I really knew nothing about being a "mom." I never had a pet growing up. It was on-the-job training.

I decided to take two female companion cats. Their photos called out to me. They looked so sweet. They were rescued from an outdoor colony in 2008, both pregnant and ready to deliver. A year later and still looking for their forever home, they and many other cats needed a temporary home. They were being evicted from a renovated barn donated to the organization. The owners were getting divorced, and the property sold. Kim Carrafiello, the Adoption Director, asked if I could help out in an emergency, and I agreed.

As I waited patiently for Kim to arrive, I paced the house, nervous and excited at the same time. This was a life-changing event for me. Most of the pet owners I spoke with were lifers. They were raised with them, and when they became adults, it was a natural progression to adopt or foster. I was single, used to setting my own schedule, responsible for only me. I was becoming a first-time "parent," and started to think I was in over my head.

Kim finally arrived with two large carriers. She entered the bedroom, setting them down side by side. She retrieved their food, litter, and box from her car and closed the door. She told me to sit quietly on the floor and observe. Delilah, on the left, was very quiet. Willie, short for Wilhelmina, was chirping like a baby bird. Kim opened the carrier doors very slowly. Delilah came out first. A black and white short-haired Tuxedo, she was lean but muscular, with beautiful aquamarine eyes. She looked at us, surveyed the room, and quickly scooted under the bed. Willie was next. A black and white long-haired Tuxedo, she was the complete opposite. She was pudgy with a white streak across her face that reminded me of the main character from Phantom of the Opera. She had one good eye, the other closed shut, damaged in a fight when she was living outside. As she slowly emerged, I immediately fell in love with her. In an instant she was gone and under the bed to join Delilah.

Later that evening I went to check on them. They were still under the bed. The food wasn't eaten, the litter box unused. I was concerned that something was wrong. Lynn Morchel, the president and founder of the rescue organization, told me to be patient and give it some time. They need to adjust to their new surroundings, she said. Kim said they should be ready to come out in a day or two. I continued to check on them every few hours, sticking my head under the bed and letting them hear the sound of my voice. At one point Delilah, who was now positioned at the foot of the bed, put her paw on my glasses. I don't think she was trying to hurt me, maybe just telling me I was invading her space.

Eventually, they did venture out, but when I entered the room they quickly retreated. After several days, I decided to sit in the room for longer periods of time in hopes they would approach me. Holding pieces of turkey in my hands did the trick. The bonding process began. The following week I opened the door and supervised their exploring the rest of the house. By the end of April they had settled in nicely. We were ready to be a family. They were becoming my two best girls.

In January 2010 Willie had a routine check-up and everything was fine. Two days later she was bleeding from the same side of her face as the damaged eye. I brought her back to the animal hospital for another exam. She had an infection that was massive and widespread throughout her head. It was serious and life-threatening. The infected area needed to be drained. If she didn't make significant improvement over the weekend, she most likely would be euthanized. Willie was one tough cookie. She survived. She needed additional care, and Kim thought it best for Willie to stay with her for a month or so while she recuperated.

Unfortunately, this was the first of many infections she would endure. In September 2011 Willie had surgery to remove the damaged eye. The consensus was the eye was causing the infections. Additionally, she had puncture wounds on that side of the face, possibly caused by a cat bite when she was living at the barn. We thought we were finally home free.

In the spring of 2012 both Willie and Delilah developed liver failure. Both were nursed back to health with feeding tubes and medication by Ashley Skidmore, a former vet technician and friend of Kim's. She was a lifesaver. Without her expertise and commitment they would not have survived. They were returned to me the end of June, healthy and happy. The cause of their illness is still unknown. Willie continued to have infections in 2013 and 2015. I moved and had work done in the new home, which may have triggered the episodes. She needs a quiet environment with no stress.

Sadly, in September 2014 Delilah became ill. It happened quickly and without warning. She had fluid in her chest and was having difficulty breathing. Rather than have her suffer, and in consultation with Kim and the doctor, the decision was made to euthanize her. Willie was still not alone. Jezabel, one of my outdoor cats I brought inside in August 2011 due to an upper respiratory infection, was there for Willie to "torment." Willie loves to tease and play. Jezabel would rather be an only "child." They've learned to tolerate each other. As I sit in my recliner it's snuggle time: Jezabel cuddling real close with her head tucked under my chin, Willie on my lap kneading my legs like a baker making bread. I'm content and so are they — me and my two best girls.

Russell's Story

By Amy Goodusky

Every cat I've had has come to me by accident. Russell, an orange and white cat of unknown breeding, arrived in April of 2007. My last cat, Kenneth, died on Good Friday. I was unable to stand even one day in a catless household. The day afterward, the Saturday before Easter, I hijacked my friend Suzanne, who is a dog person but nevertheless willing to give moral support, and went to the Humane Society.

The cat section was overloaded. I saw Russell right away. He was in a cage, by himself, in the far upper right at the entrance to the shelter. His markings were captivating. His eyes were yellow. He looked sweet, and a little forlorn.

I kept looking, feeling I couldn't simply take the first cat I saw. There were a couple of tuxedo cats that looked like characters. I considered them. Russell won. I went back to his cage. There was a note on a blue-lined index card describing his circumstances. He was nine years old. The note went on to describe that, like me, Russell was recently bereaved. He had been surrendered to a humane society when his owner died. Apparently, there was no one to take him. This sealed my decision. We would heal from our recent losses together.

I stopped a volunteer to tell her my choice. She frowned.

"Oh, Russell, he's not good with people," she said. "He's very stand-off-ish. Why don't you think about taking BW? He's really friendly!" She brought me over to BW's cage.

"He'd be a great cat for you," she said.

I was skeptical. I looked at BW. He was black and white and skinny. I hadn't noticed him on my earlier tour of the cages. He looked young. Actually, he looked like a handful. Kenneth had been older when I got him. BW was a year old. Russell was more mature. He was still my first choice.

The first volunteer disappeared while I eyeballed BW.

Another volunteer appeared at the cage. She pulled me away.

"You don't want that cat, BW," she whispered urgently. "He's crazy!"

Suzanne, who had been looking at the puppies, returned to the cat section.

I told her about the workers' comments. Suzanne encouraged me to audition Russell. I went back to the desk. The original volunteer, the one who had tried to dissuade me, looked disappointed. She shook her head as I filled out the paperwork.

"He's really very antisocial," she said dourly, as she led me to the bonding room to meet Russell.

In the bonding room were the two volunteers, me, and Suzanne. The room smelled of disinfectant and hopeful excitement. We could hear meowing and barking and the sounds of hard toenails on the linoleum. The door opened.

Russell was in a volunteer's arms. He looked nervous and quizzical, like a child at the pediatrician's office. The volunteer shut the door behind her. The first volunteer was poised to strike. She was gearing up for a big "I told you so," when the third volunteer put Russell on the floor. He looked at us, sniffed the air twice, ran across the room, and jumped onto my lap.

"Sold," I said.

"There's your boy!" Suzanne said.

The first volunteer looked disgusted. The second volunteer looked triumphant. Russell purred. He was beautiful.

The volunteers gave me a carrier, several days' supply of food, and a rabies tag. The first volunteer had disappeared again. I paid the adoption fee. Russell looked anxious to leave. We carried him to the car.

"That was interesting," I said.

Suzanne commented that Russell was an unusual name for a cat. On the day before Easter, she was contemplating chocolate, along with the rest of us secular types. She thought for a moment.
"I think he should be called...Russell Stover!" she said.

It stuck.

It was a bright, sunny Saturday. We drove home and let Russell out of the carrier. He immediately ran upstairs and under the bed. When he emerged three days later, after failing to respond to Bumble Bee tuna, roast chicken, or catnip, he seemed to have decided that he was home. Russell was never what I would have called antisocial. He remained very selective about those he would approach, however, and could not be persuaded to warm up to anyone who did not pass his personal test of integrity. I am grateful to have made the grade.

Russell lived nine more happy years. I called the Humane Society to tell them how well he was doing shortly after I brought him home. The worker who answered the phone told me that he would have been humanely destroyed on the Monday after Easter. There are no real accidents in this life.

The Saga of Sewer Kitty

By Joanne Farley

Hi! My name is Sewer Cat (Sewki for short), and I want to tell you about my exciting rescue from what would have been certain death.

It was a sunny June morning about three years ago when a woman who was out walking along the street of a local development heard some mewing. She followed the sound to a storm drain on the side of the road and peering into the grating, saw me—a tiny 24-ounce gray and white tabby kitten—squawking my head off. I was stuck down there not knowing where I was, how I got there, and how/if I'd ever get out. She ran to the closest home. A couple responded to her incessant knocking, and she explained the situation, noting she didn't have her cell to call the police. She and the man went to the drain. I promptly cranked up again to let them know I was stuck down there and very scared. The man noted he would handle the situation.

His wife called the Animal Control Officer asking for assistance. Well, the request fell on deaf ears with the uncaring guy saying I was probably part of a wild mom's litter as those kinds of cats often give birth in drain pipes since they are quiet, secluded spots, and he refused to help. In the meantime the man went to work, but kept checking on me later that day and the next morning, too. Needless to say, I was still ranting. Next, his wife went to the local Municipal building and demanded someone be sent to rescue me. Not ten minutes later the Roads Supervisor pulled into the driveway.

After checking on me again, the Roads Supervisor and homeowner devised a plan. The supervisor would use a huge crowbar to pry up the heavy drain grating, and the other man would reach down into the dark cavern and scoop me up in his pool net, pulling me to safety. Well, the first part went well, but I managed to dodge the net, as (silly me) I panicked and ran the length of the pipe across the street underground. At this point the rescuers took a break, not wanting to frighten me more. But in about thirty minutes they heard my squawks again (I was getting hoarse for sure). I had run back across the drain pipe to the original spot. I have to say by this time I was feeling kind of frantic. While the guys were scratching their heads about what to do next, some neighbors appeared with a Havahart trap (used to capture animals humanely) and put tuna in it. It was lowered down to that dark, awful spot, and in a few minutes, wonder of wonders, they had me in it, since I was starving. Hey, I was just so thrilled to be out of that scary place, eating food and seeing the sun!!

At this point the homeowner took me in his arms and packed me off to the vet. Of course I had ear mites and a major tummy infection (I hadn't eaten in days). Oh, I should mention another rescue, Vespa, a black cat, had lived there a couple of years before I arrived. And, as I had to take meds to fix me, I was segregated in a huge cage in the garage for some days. Oh, and as you might imagine, I was quite hoarse for a time. At quarantine's end, I got to go inside the house. Needless to say, my new fur sister viewed me as a major intruder and continues to do so to the present. Now I am a large (13 lbs.), lovely cat outweighing Vespa by 20%. But erf! I haven't got that figured out yet, and gee, she's so intimidating in many ways.

But I am so very thankful these people gave me a forever home, where I am happy, warm, and well cared for. Oh yeah, I have to visit the vet annually for a checkup, but that's not too bad. She is pleased with me, noting I'm eating and drinking well. Finally, if not rescued and adopted, I would have surely died, and now, well, I have the good life…

Second Chance

By Loren Spiotta-DiMare

My uncle, though a gentle and sensitive man, was not noted for his love of animals. Thus it came as no surprise when she paid her first visit one warm summer evening that he gave strict orders: We were "not to feed the cat." If insulted by his indifference, she showed no signs. In fact, she lay contentedly on the front porch until she was ready to move on.

The next day she appeared again. Bathing in the rays of the afternoon sun, she meowed softly when someone approached, yet did nothing further to encourage introductions. In a short time she was off again, only to return the following day. "I hope no one has been feeding that cat!" my uncle spoke sternly to all within earshot. "After all, she must belong to someone. It would be selfish and unfair to let her stay here." Elizabeth, his youngest, giggled softly. "I'm serious. We are not going to keep that cat!" The final word had been spoken, or so he thought.

The uncommonly attractive Calico, with yellowish gray-green eyes, continued her daily visits. Someone had given her a leftover fish chowder, and she was not one to overlook a charitable gesture. Then one afternoon she disappeared. "Probably returned to her own home," my uncle logically surmised. His relief was short lived.

A week later, one very independent cat returned, and this time she had no intention of leaving; every attempt to find her owners failed. Thus, once allowed inside the house, Quiquai, as she had been christened, captured the hearts of us all. Well, almost all. My uncle refused to give into her beguiling charm. He did his best to ignore her. Unconcerned by his indifference, she simply stayed out of his way. Eight-year-old Elizabeth, on the other hand, was delighted with the newest member of the family. She marveled at Quiquai's uncanny intelligence. After the cat had been out playing in the yard, she'd come to the front door and meow to be let in. If this failed, she'd jump and paw at the mail slot knowing full well that the clatter of metal would certainly get a response. When it did not she knew her family was out of earshot, which meant they were in the den. In that case she'd scamper to the far side of the house to investigate. If the light was on (a guarantee someone was there), she'd jump to the window's ledge and paw at the window. This method never failed to get attention.

Shortly she'd be beside the fire, daintily licking her paws. After she had lived with her new family for over a year, Quiquai disappeared. It was a stormy afternoon—everyone was sure she'd run off to find protection from the rain. Yet when she did not reappear that evening, all were concerned. After two days, Elizabeth was truly alarmed. She combed the streets, searching frantically for her lost pet. As the days wore on, she tried to accept the obvious: Quiquai would not return. Her father consoled her: "I'm sure she's alright, Liz. She probably went to find her original owners." "But why?" Liz questioned.

"She's been with us for so long. Why would she leave us now?"
"I don't know, honey, she was always very independent."

Thirteen days after Quiquai vanished, my uncle went to his guest house to connect a hose to water his garden. As he unlocked the front door, a very frightened, skinny but terribly relieved Quiquai jumped into his arms. Despite their former indifference Qui appeared convinced he had come to the cottage solely to save her. It was a deed she would never forget.

My uncle, at first startled by the cat's presence, wondered how she had gotten in and, more important, how she survived her ordeal. My aunt remembered showing the guest house to prospective renters the day Qui disappeared. To escape the rain she must have slipped in unnoticed. How she survived without food or water would never be known.

Elizabeth was so happy to have the cat back again she gave little thought to the circumstances that kept her away. Quiquai, however, was strangely affected by the incident. Of course she could not comprehend why she was trapped or possibly know if she would ever be free again. But she would always remember who rescued her. From the moment my uncle opened the front door she refused to leave his side. She followed his every step. She sat by him as he did chores. When he watched television she'd climb onto his chest and fall asleep, feeling safe and secure. Her indifference had changed to devotion.

My uncle could no longer ignore the gentle creature who so obviously adored him. He finally began to realize and appreciate her as the intelligent animal she was.

Of course there were times when he became furious with her. One Thanksgiving, for example, when my family had just finished a huge meal and settled into the living room to have coffee, I excused myself to make a phone call. As I reached the kitchen, Quiquai leapt to the counter to feast on the leftover turkey. Certain this was not acceptable behavior but not sure how to handle it, I called out, "Uncle Roland, do you let your cat jump on the counter and eat leftovers?" Above the laughter I heard him say "of course not" as he ran into the kitchen. "Bad Girl," he raised his voice so the cat would know he was serious, "you know you're not allowed on the counter, get down from there." Aware that she was in trouble, but too delighted with her find, Quiquai refused to move. He hoisted her into the air and placed her on the floor. Then he gave her a small portion of the turkey. "She knows I'd give her some. I don't know why she jumped up here."

"I guess she couldn't wait," I replied.

"That's no reason to disobey the rules," then in a softer tone, "She really is a smart cat. Did I ever tell you what she does when she wants to come in from outside?" I listened intently, trying to suppress a grin. That cat had certainly won her way into the heart of a man who "didn't care for animals."

Epilogue: Although this story has a happy ending, many cats who are allowed to roam free are not so lucky. Unlimited numbers of free-roaming cats meet tragic deaths beneath the wheels of cars, are terrorized by dogs, threatened by disease, and breed indiscriminately, adding to the pathetic pet overpopulation in this country.

Cats can live contented and much safer lives completely inside. Or they may be trained to walk in a harness on leash to enjoy the outdoors.

We Are Dog People

By Tracey Romano Grant

A tale of Smokey, our loving Spirit Animal who happens to be a cat

"**W**hy can't we get another dog?" chimed the people of the house. "We don't have a fenced-in yard, and no one will clean up after it," I replied. "How about a cat?" the plea escalated, and so did my negativity. I continued my rant, "I have allergies, I don't want a litter box, they shed, cats are not affectionate, and besides that, we are dog people!"

Does this conversation sound familiar? Without a doubt, this family was "Team Dog." We had previously had beagles, and now a seven-pound Pappion named Jack was "Head of Security" at our house. No one, including us, could enter the home without him barking bloody murder. Small and mighty, he had an attitude and pretty much had bitten every guest who had crossed our threshold. He was supposed to be a lap dog for me but hated being held. We loved him, and he was all Momma here could handle. That was about to change. Enter Smokey!

Our emerald-eyed feline was rescued from the Common Sense for Animals shelter in Warren County, New Jersey. Her arrival was bittersweet, and she came with a little emotional baggage including her Shih Tzu sister Muffin.

My amazing cousin (and several years later her grieving, loving husband) tragically passed away relatively early in life. They were survived by many, including a much-adored son, and two pets. With a home now empty and son away at college, the animals were quickly removed and taken to the closest shelter.

It is difficult to focus when tragedy strikes, but I knew as the geographically nearest relative I had to get those animals back. Their son would want to be with the pets that he loved, now more than ever. He would need some connection to his parents. I started the drive out to this unknown, remote, country shelter. Somehow, I managed to load a very annoyed cat and terrified small dog into the carriers. "I must be out of my mind," I thought to myself as I started home. I prayed that my allergies would not kick in. I prayed Jack would not freak when I walked in with these new guests.

None of that mattered. I remember when their son was reunited with his pets in my car. I could see he was clearly attached to this loving feline, and he would never let go of her. After some discussion, we decided that college was no place for a pet, so I offered to care for Smokey. His aunt would take the little dog for now.

The rest is a happy ending. We have loved this crazy kitty for over a year. He is especially attached to our daughter and is her constant companion. Unlike my "lap dog," Smokey loves to be held, pet, and nap right on top of you. I think Jack has accepted that there is a "new sheriff in town" as they are in constant surveillance of the front door together. Our relatives are able to visit her here in Long Valley whenever they want.

We were dog people. But now we are cat people, too. This affectionate, grey, slightly pudgy fur ball has a great soul that keeps the memory and spirit of his first family alive.

We were team dog, and now we are team cat, too. You can feel the divine presence of our loved ones through Smokey, our Spirit Animal, in her mesmerizing eyes and warm cuddles every day.

The litter box is full, there is hair on every bed, but with two teenagers here it's hard to notice the difference anyway. I think I will go find Smokey and take a nap with her since my cat allergies do not exist anymore. I know I can find her on whichever bed has the stream of sunlight right now, or waiting patiently on the staircase. She is waiting to be cuddled—the lap dog I always wanted who happens to be a cat.

Tails' Tales

By Cheryl Slegers

Physician, theologian, musician, and philosopher Albert Schweitzer said, "There are two means of refuge from the miseries of life… music and cats." I found this quote on a coffee and tea-stained, well-used aromatic coaster, which sits on my human Grandma's smooth and cracked maple desk top. (I understand this desk was her mom's desk, inherited years ago…maybe a future tale to tell). Of course, I can't read the words on the coaster, but my catly intuition tells me how much she connects with its message and, thus, to me. We relate on an unspoken level and totally understand each other.

I love this man, Albert Schweitzer, for honoring and giving me and my fellow feline's purr-pose in this messy world. He has charged me to offer sanctuary, protection, and healing from life's sorrows, grief, suffering, anguish, agony, sadness, and pain. That's a very tall order, but it suits me well, as I have mastered the art of living…a very simple formula consisting of napping, playing, eating, cuddling, easily walking away and hiding out for a while, if solitude is what I need or want (no excuses necessary), exploring, patiently waiting (except when I'm hungry), listening intently, and running like a bat out of hell…just because. And, I get the music part…it intrigues me…for what is music but patterns of sounds and silence expressing feelings that words can't always capture. Right up my alley.

Grandma has decided to use me, with my permission of course, as the spokes-cat for her stories that have been brewing for years in journals stored methodically in boxes in a closet. She has already told some stories through lyrics and music, and now wants to continue the journey through storytelling and share it with her family, and whoever else wants to listen. So, I suppose, a brief introduction is in order and what my qualifications are for this task of telling her tales.

My name is Tails (originally Tiger, just for the record). I have an extremely disproportionably long tail, which is my nemesis, my Achilles heel, as it were. I am normally an affectionate, playful, and companionable cat but, periodically and unpredictably, I get very ferocious with hissing and growling and chase madly after the suspicious and intruding appendage, acting out some kind of wild fantasy jungle battle. It's scary for me and anyone else in the vicinity. We all believe, and the vet concurs, that it's some kind of seizure and so we let it run its course—a minute or two—and then resume life as usual (as if life around here is anything usual.)

It was love at first sight. Swishing my magnificent tail gracefully back and forth and gazing adoringly up at her with my sparkling intense cat eyes was more than she could take. After some business preliminaries, you know, the paperwork documentation saying I was who I was and they were who they said they were, exchange of some fees, and a promise to return at puberty to get spayed, and I was regally carried out in a crate to newfound freedom...an hour's ride to the country to meet more new family.

Upon arrival, I excitedly leaped from the crate. I'm an expert leaper, and LOVE diving and soaring through the air artfully and elegantly every chance I get. With unbelievable poise, balance, and accuracy, I can make a single jump from the floor up to seemingly insurmountable heights. My human family is absolutely amazed at my prowess and grace. I have impressed them with the great distance I can spring from the top of the washing machine in one room to the counter in the kitchen, or from the floor in the mud room through a cracked window into the bathroom when I was recuperating from a surgery and supposed to be quietly resting (more later).

Anyway, I'm on a tangent. Back to my first night in my new digs. Bounding ecstatically from my cage, I jumped on top of the kitchen counter and hid behind the microwave as I was met by the biggest, roundest, most hypnotic pair of eyes I had ever encountered and the wildest warning hiss imaginable. A huge, magnificent, mostly bright white, splashed with gray mixed breed domestic short hair, weighing in at about fifteen pounds (let me mention here that I was only about seven and a half pounds back then) ferocious cat blocked my entrance. I had just met my step-cat sister, Kiki.

Right from the start, I could see she had issues. I was used to the hustle and bustle of the animal shelter where I was surrounded by other feline playmates and loved the camaraderie. I could see immediately that Kiki was not so predisposed. I learned later that she, too, was rescued after being found in the woods in Pennsylvania by a couple of cat lovers who already had a family of eight cats. From day one this sisterhood of eight never took very kindly to Rosie, as she was called for unknown reason in those days. Apparently, out of necessity because she was shunned by this established household, Rosie was banished, exiled to the bedroom and bathroom areas of the house where she, I have heard, was content to play with her toys, scratch on her scratch pad, and slide down and around the sleek dry bathtub, habits she still has to this day. Since her rescue family of cats wouldn't accept her, although knowing her the way I know her today I'm sure she didn't help the situation, she was put up for adoption. Grandma was musical friends with the family and drove from New Jersey to Pennsylvania with another singer friend to meet Rosie. Grandma was surprised at the size of Rosie (large for the kitten she was supposed to be) but found her gorgeous, a little distant and skittish but gorgeous nontheless. Rosie was soon loaded into the car and proceeded to talk from her carry cage all the way back to Jersey. That was back around 2008, two years before my arrival.

Her majestic (even at that kitten age) entrance into her new home was uneventful as Rosie perused her surroundings with an aloof, tentative, distant air. Her infamous scratch pad, water bowl, and food dish, packed and carried with her from her foster Pennsylvania home, were placed on the floor in the kitchen next to the humming refrigerator. She immediately jumped onto the pad and started her meditative moves, kneading and scratching to relieve any tension she was most likely holding in those broad shoulders. A chirpy, squeaky sound escaped from her very pink mouth, and she was instantly renamed Kiki, Japanese for squeak.

After this less than cordial greeting from Kiki, I hung out behind that microwave for what seemed an eternity as she, in no uncertain terms, let me know this was HER home. In her tricky, stealthy, investigator-Kiki way, she feigned boredom with me. She has a way of disappearing, just around the corner, and spying ever so cleverly on the goings-on in the household. Heaven help any mouse that happens by. Believe me, I know. Since moving in we've had our share of hunting expeditions and actually work quite well together as a mousing team, much to the horror of the humans in this family.

Anyway, after assessing my chances of getting around her, I summoned up the courage to explore later in the evening. Darting out of her way, I escaped to another room where I discovered my human dad's (Grandma's son) armoire. I sprang onto the top shelf and snuggled into his folded shirts to stay out of harm's way and get a good night's sleep, a talent I still have to this day. There was no way Kiki was getting into this tight spot. She can run and jump but not nearly as swiftly or daringly as I can. She makes a great blocker but doesn't have my speed and athleticism. Yes, I would get a good night's sleep, let Kiki do her thing, and then begin this new chapter of my life with my adoptive family in the morning. To paraphrase a line from one of Grandma's favorite movies, Casablanca, "Kiki, Mom, Dad, Grandma, Grandpa...I think this is the beginning of a beautiful friendship."

That One

By MaryAnn Sauer

W
e had traveled there together, the four of us: my husband, our four-year-old son, my ninety-four-year-old mom, and me. It was to be just a simple, pleasant day's outing and the opportunity to see the different varieties of cats. No concerns. There were no plans to find a new cat. We already had two. And beyond that, I had no desire to buy a purebred cat. And if I did, I won't start there. Many years before I had been to my first cat show. I had been merely curious. My interest was met with such sneering snobbery; I came away thinking "those people really don't care about cats." I have had cats my entire life. Only once did I seek a breeder, in order to get a specific type of cat; it was a regrettable experience. But that is another story.

So we went to the "East Coast Premier Cat Show." The entrance was jammed. What was wrong? Was the place this popular a venue? As I got through the doors, I noticed them: multiple stacked, mis-matched, old, well-worn cages and carriers. Where were the velvet couches? Ah, no. The foyer was populated with rescue groups and shelters looking to place the less desirable, the less fortunate, and the infinitely more affordable. This was a new experience. What a great idea! All these homeless, forgotten, unwanted cats and all these "crazy-for-cats" folks. This is perfect! What a great idea! Oh, so many cats. There had to be ten or twelve organizations here. You had to snake your way through the disarranged groups. Crowds. More cats in cages. It was hard to move. Like New Year's Eve in Times Square. But a different sound, though; not so joyous. A different smell, like, "I'm waiting, again. How long will I have to wait, this time?" In a word, it was overwhelming.

Most of the cage occupants were awake, curiously staring at the human flood, ebbing and flowing around the cages. None of them appeared too hopeful. They didn't dare. They had seen all this before, so why get your hopes up for no reason?

Somehow, my family had split up in the chaos. My mom had taken my son and gone off in one direction. My husband? I had no idea where he had gone. I found myself floating, no particular course, periodically thrown up on the shore of another of the endless collection of beautiful, abandoned, lost, and forgotten creatures whose lives had somehow become discounted. Reading some of the "bios" attached to the cages did not go a long way to comfort one. What was I doing here?! I suddenly became sickened by the thought that I had come to see the "fancy cats." No, life is not that simple.

I turned, thinking I would just leave. It was really a mistake coming here. I turned looking for the way out, and in doing so caught sight of a tiny ball of black fur squished up in the back corner of a cage, which was stacked behind other empty cages. "Oh God, that one has given up completely," I found myself thinking. I edged closer. I was being pulled against my will. I knew better! There was a dirty, tattered sheet of paper pinned on the cage. It was turned, the blank page facing the reader.

I reached out, and I turned it over. It read:

"Elvira has been at our shelter for over two years now. She was brought in with her kittens. They were all adopted out. About three to four months into her stay, an almost dead mother cat was brought in with her kittens. Elvira 'adopted' them and nursed them. They were adopted out. Elvira still lives at the animal shelter in a cage she shares with two other cats."

That was it. Over two years later that cat is still at the animal shelter, waiting to be adopted. No one wanted her.

I had, initially, the impulse to run. I could not begin to calculate the emotional investment. I had to get out of there!

Not long after I ran into my husband. He was similarly overwhelmed and tired, and we had not even gotten to the "Cat Show" yet. He looked at me, sensing my discomfort.

Distractedly, I murmured, "Sorry. I am really haunted by something here." Actually, it was two. Two stories were shaking me to the core. "Did you read the bio of the eighteen-year-old cat? Son leaves for college, and mom dumps the eighteen-year-old cat at the animal shelter?"

"Yeah. Saw that," my husband slowly responded. "Like, who is going to adopt an eighteen-year-old cat?"

"More like what kind of a mom dumps a kid's eighteen-year-old pet?" I shuddered. How did she feel about the eighteen-year-old son?

My husband said, "It's that other one that bothers me."

Oh. That one. I knew intuitively which one "That One" was. That little ball of black fur squished against the mesh back wall of that cage: "Why even bother looking at them. Why get my hopes up? No one wants me. No one will ever pick me."

He pointed in the direction where my brain calculated was the precise location of the despondent cat.

"It is so sad! What a story she has. And you know she must have a good heart, to have adopted those other kittens and nurse them as her own, and..." My voice trailed off. I saw the look on his face. Was there a trace of pleading in my tone?

He said nothing, but the look on his face was: "Stop. Stop now. You know we can't. We already have two. Another means more food, more litter, more vet bills." All this summed up in a facial expression. But I know he is right. I have a four-year-old, a ninety-four-year-old, two cats, a house, and all the obligations and responsibilities and work—not to mention my family's fear that I will eventually be the subject of a Breaking News story, a SWAT team accompanying the ASPCA as they cart out van loads of carriers, long tails and pointed ears sticking out of the crates, being removed by distressed workers and disgusted neighbors adding commentary. No. I can't let that happen. Forget about it. Let someone else worry about it. I bet you, before this Cat Show is over today, some wonderful person will just scoop her up and take her away! An older person, recently bereaved, with an empty apartment and lots of time; what a great life she is going to have in her new place. I saw it all: rooms, hallways, worn Persian carpets, pale light streaming in through not the cleanest windows. A big old bed, a thick down quilt with the accumulated scents of home: the roasted foods of treasured recipes, the residents past and present. Contentment, companionship—the bonding of lonely souls until the end. I had worked it all out. It was wonderful. She was going to have a happy ending after all.

We went to see the perfect, pampered cats. They make eye contact with no one. They are so accustomed to admiration. I don't remember a single one. And so we returned home. And I absolutely did not allow myself to think about it. The next day, a Sunday, I had a fleeting memory of the good life that I had created for that tiny squished ball of fur. My husband and I never mentioned it. You wouldn't think we had even been to the Cat Show. Monday, something bothered me. I started to brood. Suppose the new situation had not worked out? Suppose the cat had to be returned because it was too much of a burden for that elderly person? Suppose they had just dragged that cat back to the shelter and stuffed her back into her cell with the other two cats? I found myself obsessing about this cat. A cat whom I had never really seen, because she was squished up against the wire mesh of a cage, staring at a blank brick wall. This was getting ridiculous! I jumped when the phone rang. It was my husband. I had to get my act together because I was now determined to broach the subject.

"Hi! I'm glad you called. There is something I want to talk to you about..."

"Okay, but before you do, I would like you to call that rescue place, you know, the one with that cat..."

"What!?"

"You know, maybe you could call them and see if she has been adopted?"

"Are you kidding me? I mean, are you serious?"

"Yes. It has been on my mind..."

"But that's what I wanted to talk to you about! That cat. It has been on my mind, and I can't let it go."

"Me either."

It turns out the elderly person with the cozy apartment had never shown up. As a matter of fact, no one had shown interest in that cat. That cat was very much available.

It has been twelve years now; we spend a lot of time together. I try not to wash the windows too often because the bright light bothers her eyes. After I straighten the sheets, I pull the thick down quilt up over my pillow. She jumps up into the bed a little later on, turns several small circles to squish the covers down, and then squeezes herself up against the pillow. But she always faces out now, looks out, and smiles.

The Cat From Beijing

By Apara Mahal Sylvester

There is a saying in the United States that proclaims the dog to be man's best friend. Firstly, I am a woman, so immediately I am excused from the norm. Secondly, all my life I have had a particular affinity toward members of the feline species, so again I beg to be pardoned. Lastly, I'm not a dog person.

It's as simple as that.

Being the adventurous type, I decided to try my luck at working in China—Beijing, to be specific. Moving to Beijing, as I so boldly did, involved some sacrifices, as many things in life do. One of these sacrifices was the separation from my beloved cat Maggie. You see, Maggie never showed her love for me in a conventional cat way. The occasional bite and swat of her razor-sharp claws were substitutes for purring and sitting on my lap. Still, she was mine. I loved her, faults and all. All of us have our faults, don't we? But I had to follow my dreams of going to China. So, left in the capable hands of my parents, we sadly parted. Well, I was sad. Maggie was indifferent. She was never one to be good at goodbyes.

After getting adjusted to living in my new world, I began to long for some companionship as I was living alone. Another human was out of the question. Humans are too complex sometimes. In China, man's best friend quickly becomes man's best entree, and you already know my opinion of dogs. I once relented and bought lovebirds, but they died within twenty-four hours of each other (no reflection on my own love life). A cat crossed my mind a few times, but I just told myself no. So I remained companionless.

For those of you who aren't familiar with Beijing life, food is a major part of the culture. Remember when your mother told you to finish your Brussels sprouts because there were starving children in China? Well, with restaurants coming out of your ears from all angles, I can hardly see how this could ever be possible. I still wonder how they all manage to stay in business.

Restaurants in Beijing don't make a big issue of trying to attract customers as they sometimes do in the USA. In a land of one billion people, a restaurant going out of business is about as likely as Elvis losing his title as King of Rock and Roll. However, some restaurants do make a point of displaying their menu items in a live, visual form outside. A common sight is cages stuffed with chickens that look like survivors of war, fish in tanks that look like the losers of the war with the chickens, and some other displays as well. Nothing out of the ordinary to an American's taste buds. But keep in mind my comment about man's best entree.

On one of my ventures out to our Chinese version of ShopRite®, I spied something quite out of the ordinary outside a local restaurant. To my horror, above a cage of chickens from a recent war sat a kitten, which was obviously that evening's blue plate special. It was a sorrowful sight to see: no water, a measly chicken bone to pick on, and totally trapped.

Now all of you know how I feel about cats. Well, what happened next could've come straight out of a supermarket romance novel: The kitten gazed at me with sorrowful, longing eyes. My heart skipped a beat, and I gazed back with mutual longing. It let out a pitiful meow. Then it happened. The moment we long for all our lives. It was love. So unexpected, so perfect, so right. That meow said it all. "Oh beautiful Goddess, save me from this wretched fate of mine. Take me, and my devotion will be yours forever."

Ok, maybe the Goddess part is overdoing it just a bit. But this is my story, so just keep on reading.

I was appalled at the sight, but I knew what had to be done. I had a mission. I raced home, made a couple of phone calls to get authorization to take on a roommate, gathered up all my hard-earned cash, and off I went to the rescue, hoping the little soul wasn't already being served as the main course.

To my relief, the kitten was just as uncooked as I left it. I quickly summoned the waitress out, expressed my intentions in Chinese (which was as pitiful as the kitten), and for the cost of a true blue plate special ($6.25 to be exact), the kitten was mine. My soulmate. I bundled the kitten up in my jacket, and off we went into the sunset (well, darkness) to begin our new life together.

ShopRite® is a registered trademark of Wakefern Foodcorp.

For those of you who aren't female, there's something you need to know about the female psyche. We have this thing called "female bonding." It's when a female feels this special connection with another female so much so that you could become inseparable and lifelong friends. I just knew the bonding thing was at work here. So I named my new little girl Mimi.

My life was complete.

I had a gal pal. I had a companion. I had a cat!

Now, as all good mothers do, I took my new charge to the vet to have a checkup. Before I go on, one thing I should mention is that I am ignorant when it comes to anything other than human genitalia. Well, to my utter disbelief, the kindly Chinese vet informed me that I was the owner of a healthy MALE cat. Mimi a mister? What happened to female bonding? How could I be so wrong? Still in shock, I proceeded to take my new little boy home. A renaming ceremony was in order. Henceforth, Mimi was known as Zhang Miao.

Another lesson is in order here regarding names in China. The Chinese take much pride and care in picking a name for their child. Giving your child a name with a special, significant meaning reflects the life of the child, and sometimes their personal characteristics. Why did I choose Zhang Miao? My cat is Chinese so giving him a Chinese name seemed appropriate. Zhang is a common surname in China. Miao is pronounced the same as meow. Simple enough.

Later on, my students informed me the English translation for Zhang is paper. Well, I wouldn't say my little guy particularly likes paper. Objects that shatter and fly into a million pieces when swatted tickles his fancy more. Zhang Miao truly is a Chinese cat at heart. His love of the color red became apparent when he decorated my floor with red nail polish, bottle and all. Many a delicate trinket has been lost forever in his quests of curiosity. Whoever said that curiosity killed the cat must have been a former cat lover who owned a crystal shop. You can guess why I used the word "former." Fear not, though, Zhang Miao is still among the living.

As I stated earlier, all of us have our faults.

Zhang Miao is now a year old. He has grown into a beautiful cat of orange color with warm yellow eyes. Still, he loves to test my patience. His cravings for attention at six a.m. compete with my cravings for sleep on most mornings. He's cleverly figured out that hitting my face with his paw would surely wake me up. He's learned that teeth are a useful weapon, which he tries out on me most of the time in the most loving ways. His quests for trying to break things never fail to emerge when I'm on an important phone call. Many an eardrum has been shattered from my deafening "Zhang Miao, get down from there!"

This may not be your conventional love story, but love happens in all shapes and forms. I love Zhang Miao with all my heart. He's faithful. He gives me happiness. He is my friend. Isn't that what love is all about?

They say you can tell a lot about a person by looking into their eyes. This holds true for animals as well, even more. I see the terror when he's done something wrong. I pity the sadness as I leave for work, and I'm comforted by the joyful glimmer when I come home.

Sometimes, though not very often nowadays, I even detect a grateful look of thanks. Though we can't bond as females do, we are bonded in other ways nevertheless. He knows I'm responsible for his being alive, and he knows I'll always keep him safe from harm. I know he'll always be loyal to me. I couldn't ask any more from love. Could anyone?

The Kitty Who Came in From the Cold

By Mary L. Copper

Meet Miss Howler our feral cat who after ten years of failed attempts to get her to come in and be our house kitty finally did.

It was the January 22, 2016, blizzard that helped her make up her mind.

Howler appeared in our yard about ten years ago. She was very thin, limping, very shy and hungry. We had rescued other homeless/feral cats and kittens, so I was off to the store for a bag of cat food. She daintily ate all the food, gave a meow of thanks, and disappeared. She apparently liked our yard as she set up housekeeping in our shed (my husband put a pillow in the wagon for her), and she also enjoyed sleeping on the porch in a basket of leaves.

She appeared on the front porch every morning howling (hence her name) like a tiger. She was loud but always appreciated a full bowl.

95

Howler soon developed a cat/person relationship with my husband; there were extended conversations each morning and eventually leg rubs. I was not so lucky, but eventually she did follow me around the yard and chatter away...no touching was permitted.

My husband was calling her Howler, but she did not look or act like a boy cat (no signs of fights, etc.), and she was delicate and small and just acted like a lady. I worried about kittens and was thinking vet. We were on one of our tours of the yard, and she was rolling in the leaves showing tummy, she was definitely a lady cat, and I was relieved to see a healing incision from a kitty hysterectomy.

We really enjoyed Howler, aka KitKit, but she kept her distance and made her boundaries clear. She is very verbal and has quite a vocabulary, from sweet little mews and chirps to very loud howls, and my husband swears that he taught her to say mama. She chatted with us all the time and seemed to understand us. She always met us in the drive when we came home, and eventually an occasional ear rub was allowed.

I missed having an indoor kitty, and she was such a sweet kitty that I tried unsuccessfully to get her to come in. I could get her as far as the foyer and leave her to make herself at home. It lasted ten to fifteen minutes, and she was at the door crying and trying to get out. So she was our outdoor cat and our only cat. We made sure she was fed, safe, loved from afar, and taken care of when we were away. The neighbors got a kick out of her sitting in the drive staring down the road. She was always there to meet us no matter the time of day or weather, and we were told about us having the nerve to leave her. She survived several snow storms; she would get snowed in under the porch, and we would dig her out and dig a path around the yard for her. She made it through

96

Hurricane Sandy with no ill effects...she was gone for two days and just appeared on the porch howling for food as if nothing had happened.

Last winter when the blizzard was on its way, we put a bed, litter box, and food in the garage. On Friday, we looked all over for her and no kitty. Since she is a senior kitty, we really worried about her surviving the storm. It started snowing, and the accumulation was fast. We kept calling and looking; she did not come for supper. I was up most of the night checking the porch for her. The next morning it was still snowing, and there were three- and four-foot drifts on the porch, and a very upset little kitty howling, stuck behind a snow drift. We could not get the front door open, so my husband opened the garage door and called her. Seeing a cat jump three-foot snow drifts was an amazing and welcome sight. She was in the garage, and the first thing she did was use the litter box. She emptied her bowl and went and hid in the loft. We moved her bed to the loft and left her to adjust to her new room.

She hid in the loft for a couple of days, only coming out for food and litter box stops. I was finally successful in getting her to come down and visit. A few leg rubs and ear rubs were allowed with the usual kitty conversation.

After about a week, there was a cute little meow at the garage door, and my husband invited her in. We expected her to come in and go hide somewhere. The big surprise was that Howler stood in the living room door, and I called her and invited her up into my lap, and much to my delight she jumped up onto my lap and stayed there. She was nervous at first but eventually settled down to sleep. At first she would go back to the garage, but eventually we were able to get her to stay in the house full time, and she finally became our inside kitty. My lap is her favorite place.

She is a sweet, laid-back kitty and continues to be very talkative. She has opinions on everything, and very definite limitations. She loves to sit on my lap, petting and ear rubs are enjoyed, but there is no picking up or cuddling and, unlike most cats, she does not like boxes, bags, or getting under covers. The not liking box thing made a trip to the vet difficult, but we have a great vet hospital that makes house calls. I was a little anxious about the visit not knowing what she would do, but I was amazed. You could tell she was nervous but she was an angel, no crying, no attempted scratching or biting. The vet could not believe she had been outside for ten years. For the record, I paid for my attempts to look after her health needs by her hiding in the garage loft for the rest of the day.

She is very gentle and never scratches the furniture or walls. She is welcome to sit on the furniture and does not climb on counters or the table. She never begs for food and always gives a chirp of thanks when her bowl is filled. She still likes to go out once in a while and will howl at the door to be let out. We keep a close eye on her, and she never stays out for long. She seems to have a need to check out her yard, and she runs around like a crazy wild cat. If the weather is not acceptable to her, she will spend time running around the house growling, and she likes a game called chase the kitty and then find the kitty. I guess you can bring in the wild cat, but some of the wild stays in the cat. She really seems to understand us. When we are ready for bed, I will say "nite nite the kitty," and she will jump off my lap and meow a good night.

We are so happy to welcome her into what is now her forever home. She is a great companion and buddy. I have some bad days health-wise, and she does not leave my side. We will be sitting in our chair, and she will be asleep and will all of the sudden wake up, sit up at attention, look at me, and meow as if to say "how are you, Mama?" She tells some great stories...too bad I don't speak cat because that would mean a really neat story!

Some additional Howler information...our neighbors were very happy that she is now a house cat but unhappy with the mole population and the fact that they had a mouse in their house for the first time. When we sit in our chair with a cover, if I put my hands under the covers, she gets very upset and meows at me till I show my hands. Howler likes to play but only likes toys and the origami birds that I fold. She is afraid of the other toys like mice, balls, and ribbons. She is very fond of catnip. I would say that cats who are outside most of their lives do not have happy kitten lives like those lucky enough to be adopted when they are babies. Here is a recent first...Howler let me pick her up and give her hugs, and she did not panic...YAY!

Tiger (or Kika— Kee-KAH in Hawaiian)

By Peggy Regentine

Tiger was found on the Pali Highway, a connecting road from Honolulu to Kailua on the Hawaiian island of Oahu. Tiger and his two siblings were cuddled in a box on the side of the highway, left to survive at four weeks of age. Tiger's hyper personality must have developed from not having a mom swat him for his mischievous behavior. A friend adopted two of the three boxed kittens, and Tiger was headed for the Humane Shelter.

WAIT. I intercepted at Petland, grabbed a small cardboard box, and headed home with the little bundle of joy to show my boyfriend, Stote. The rescuer seemed well versed in kittens and said the three kittens were approximately the above-mentioned age. Tiger was pre-named by the rescuer. Tiger had a tabby coat and stripes. Being that our Tiger was female, we changed her name to Tigress. Tiger at her young age didn't seem to mind.

Two weeks passed and we decided two things: We wanted a cat able to explore the outdoors but not be an outdoor cat whose lifespan is drastically challenged. Next, we wanted to walk our kitten on a leash. So off I go to Petland for a pink harness and leash with the purpose of becoming a doting cat mama.

WAIT. I get a phone call. Can I sit down? Not knowing what to think Stote and I find a bench. The caller seemed worried that the information she was to announce would alter my feelings for our little one. She blurted out, "Tigress is not a female! Neither are his brothers!" I hear loud and clear. What? Did I hear correctly as I had been assured the rescuer knew her cat anatomy. I questioned this assessment. Are you sure? I was certain our caller had made a mistake. A bit stunned we immediately located our iPhones and Googled "sex of kittens." We found a YouTube video with a vet tech explaining how to determine the sex of a kitten. Bingo! Mr. Google is right! Without legible genitalia, the male kitten part is closer to its anus than the female. Now all the rumors of how challenging male cats are begin to conjure in our heads. Honestly, cat mama was definitely too attached to worry about the sex of the little rascal. Well, it certainly looks as if Tiger, not Tigress, was a perfect name! No more pink collars for our kitten. It is blue starting right then.

WAIT! Did I mention that I never had children? Yes, I have read that childless cat owners are the worst, absolute worst. Kellyanne Conway, the first woman to manage a winning Presidential campaign, has been criticized for being a stay-at-home mom with her favorite label as "mommy." Her response to these critiques is that these childless women post their cats on Twitter rather than their kids. I admire Kellyanne! I admire her mommy values. And yikes, I have posted Tiger on Facebook. Does that count?

Being a teacher, I also felt that Tiger needed training. I questioned Tiger's IQ as we knew nothing of his feline parents. Umm...do feral cats have brains? Luckily, we found Wayne who specializes in training cats. Wayne's expertise is unusual as dogs always seem to be the priority in research, clinics, pet stores, and training. Being a soft-spoken man, our cat trainer is perfect. Wayne comes to our first session wearing a t-shirt with a tiger imprinted on the chest. What a match! We immediately are impressed with Wayne's operant conditioning training methods: rewarding positive behavior. Looking at a training manual, this is Wayne's bible.

Event	Add or Give	Take Away or Subtract
Something Pleasant	Positive Reinforcement	Negative Punishment

PERFECT! REWARDS! Tiger has a voracious appetite and loves treats for tricks! To this day, we have trained our adopted (extremely intelligent) Tiger to sit, shake hands, go down, roll over, come up, and up higher. Yes, feral cats do have brains, do need love, and are perfect companion animals. Especially for Peggy and Stote.

Dickens and Murphy, Best Buddies

By Mary Lou Burde

I've always been a "cat person," it seems. From when I was a toddler nuzzling kittens on a farm to playing with neighborhood cats to finally having my own cats, cats have provided me with inestimable joy and affection. I've been owned by a black cat when my family lived in Argentina, and by a tabby and tuxedo cat once I acquired my own home. Currently, I share my home with my husband, George, and two remarkable orange cat brothers, Murphy and Dickens. They are the most affectionate and funny cats I've ever had, and George and I laugh at their antics every day.

I came upon these two sweethearts while volunteering at St. Hubert's Animal Welfare Center in Madison, NJ. My job was to socialize the cats who were somewhat frightened of being uprooted and housed in a strange place. What a job—I would have paid them to do it!

One day, an orange cat by the name of Orangino came running up to me as I entered the cattery. He jumped in my lap, and I looked at my fellow volunteer with wide eyes. I had lost my cat about six months earlier, and was waiting for the right cat—or the right two cats, to be specific. "He's adorable," I said, "but I'm really looking for two cats." At that comment, a staff member strolled by and said "he has a brother." Enter Sunshine, who was less gregarious but still very affectionate. Well, that was that, and I adopted them on the spot. I brought them home that day in temporary cardboard carriers. I hadn't even prepared my home with food and litter box, but that was quickly remedied. Apparently the cats had been abandoned in an apartment building when the owners vacated without them. Thankfully, the landlord knew of this and was feeding them before taking them to St. Hubert's. How could anyone leave these two??

First on my list was to change the names, as Orangino and Sunshine didn't seem to reflect their personalities. Not only that, but shortened to Gino and Sonny, they sounded like mobster cats. I named Orangino Murphy to reflect his "man-about-town" nature. Sunshine became Dickens, named after a book entitled "A Dickens of a Cat" with an orange cat on the cover very similar to Sunshine.

I adopted the boys in October 2012 and met my future husband George a few months later in January 2013. At the first date, I had to mention the cats, as any potential mate had to be a cat lover. An aversion or indifference to cats would be a definite deal-breaker! Luckily, my now-husband adored cats and missed his own cat who had passed away the previous year. Now he and I are devoted cat parents. One of Murphy's favorite routines is to follow George around in the morning until he sits down with his coffee, then jumps up and nestles in "his" position on George's arm.

They have been the most amazing cats I've ever met (biased opinion). Not ones to run FROM the doorbell as my past sweet, more shy cats had done—but they run TO the door to see who it is. They've made friends with the cable guy, contractors, friends, and neighbors, as they always want to be in on the action. Most recently Dickens followed us from room to room as a window contractor measured each window. Guess he wanted to give it his "paw of approval."

The two cats are very closely bonded. They wrestle together daily, quite roughly it seems, but they seem to love it and go back for more. They chase each other around the house, sounding like a herd of elephants. They groom each other (often ending in a wrestle), and snuggle together to nap.

Murphy has a comical personality while Dickens is more focused on getting affection, though not above a crazy race around the house with his brother. Actually, Murphy makes us laugh just looking at his goofy expression. When he's not being silly, we usually find him napping on our bed. My cat sitter says "he looks like he just got up"—well, yes, there's a reason for that. When he plays, he has great fun chasing imaginary mice and dashing away from us, wanting us to follow. When he's really wound up, he runs around with his tail hooked in the air.

Dickens is "the greeter." He is always at the door where we enter, meowing his hello with his "where have you been?" expression. He loves attention. He is so mellow that we can pick him up from where he is lying and he stays flat in our arms like a platter. Dickens has also developed a routine of crying incessantly until I pick him up and sling him over my shoulder like a baby. Instant contentment! The purr starts and the paws start kneading the air. When he gets especially happy, his tail fluffs up like a bottle brush. Dickens' other noisy routine is carrying around a toy in his mouth about half his size, simultaneously crying. This can go on for ten minutes or more. We call it Dickens' singing. He eventually brings the toy to us and lays it at our feet. AND—Dickens is the second of my cats that enjoys retrieving. I throw an object (cat toy, wadded up piece of paper) for him to chase, and he runs back with it to me. However, being a cat, he doesn't actually put the object within reach. I must get up and move a few feet to pick it up and throw it again. He loves this game, and I tire of it before he does. He's also expert at knocking things off surfaces (we thought we could hire him out as a busboy) and at climbing as high as possible, including the top of our kitchen cabinets.

Our home and routine center around these important family members, of course. They have a large cat tree from which they can observe birds, squirrels, chipmunks, deer, and all manner of wildlife— from the safety of the enclosed porch. It's their favorite place to hang out in good weather. In the winter, they've become partial to the fireplace, getting as close as possible to the source of heat. Their fur gets so warm I'm amazed they don't self-combust! And ALWAYS, our laps are a favored place.

One summer, after a very difficult year caring for critically ill parents, my back decided it had had enough and went into a spasm severe enough to land me in bed for weeks. The boys stayed by my side almost continually, keeping me company and lifting my spirits.

We really cannot imagine our lives without these two endearing creatures. It's hard to express how tightly they have woven themselves into our home and hearts. We celebrate them every day.

A Tale of Two Kitties

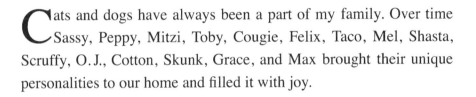

By Laureen Berg

Cats and dogs have always been a part of my family. Over time Sassy, Peppy, Mitzi, Toby, Cougie, Felix, Taco, Mel, Shasta, Scruffy, O.J., Cotton, Skunk, Grace, and Max brought their unique personalities to our home and filled it with joy.

Years ago, our pets were not "rescued" or "adopted." Many trips were made to the SPCA to choose a new friend. Others came from people whose pets had a litter or could no longer care for theirs.

Our last two cats were with us the longest. Skunk was an Illinois barn cat, picked from a litter in 1976. He died on Flag Day in 1993. Grace was our first "adoption," coming to us in December of 1993. She was put to sleep in the summer of 2008.

Choosing a name everyone agrees on can be difficult. A neighbor remarked how much our new kitten looked like a skunk with the white stripe running from his nose, right over the middle of his head, to his shoulders. He was mostly black, with two white front paws and

107

a white chest—and the head stripe. And so he became Skunk, a.k.a. Skunk the Cat.

Skunk never used a litter box, he would meow at the door to be let out. The longer he had to wait, the louder and more drawn out the meow. In his youth he was a real tomcat on the prowl. Two scary days we looked all over the neighborhood for him, the kids were upset that he might be lost forever. On the third day he sauntered up the driveway and meowed at the door. He was such a mess! Dirty, a cut on his paw, and one over his eye; it was obvious he'd been in a fight. We all hugged and petted, and gently tried to clean him up.

"You should see the other guy!" he seemed to say, shrugging us off. We took him to the vet where he was given antibiotics, and a wick was inserted above his eye that we would have to slide back and forth so the skin would not grow around it. Skunk was never gone overnight again, but he did come home with evidence of altercations.

In 1979 we moved to West Virginia, in a more rural neighborhood. Everybody knew everyone else's kids, but they also knew their pets. A call would come from a neighbor two streets away to let us know that Skunk was on patrol. When the kids were out playing, he would keep an eye on them; if there was yelling or crying, he would start caterwauling. When my husband and I went for a walk, we would look behind us and find him following. Sometimes I would scoop him up to carry him home, but he would have none of it. We called him the adorable twenty-pounder, his weight at his healthiest and most robust.

True to the species, he liked only being held or petted on his terms. Skunk slept on one of our beds at night, you never knew if you would find him curled at your feet in the morning. Curious, he could be found in the oddest places: an open file drawer, hanging out of a slipper, a box, or bag, and in the bass drum of my daughter's drum set.

Ornery is a good descriptor also. Skunk would lie in wait in the bushes along the front walk and attack anyone who dared to walk by. He would literally fly out of the bush and grab onto a leg or foot and bite. One evening he was sleeping in the chair next to my bed. I turned off the light to go to sleep, and minutes later he launched himself onto my head, claws out, then leapt away.

After ten years in West Virginia, we moved to Massachusetts for three years. The night we arrived, he escaped from the pet taxi and could not be found. We were going to spend the night in a hotel, but our two kids wouldn't leave the house. With movers in and out and doors open we didn't know if Skunk was hiding in the house or hitch-hiking to West Virginia.

It was a bitter cold February night that found us walking around an unfamiliar neighborhood calling for our lost cat. Exhausted, my husband and I went to the hotel, thinking what a sad way to begin a new adventure. Around 3:30 a.m. our phone rang, a scary time for a call. But it was our two teen-aged children happily crying that Skunk had appeared, meowing, from under a bed in an upstairs room.

Over the next two years Skunk became old, more lethargic. Though at times he surprised us with kitten-like antics and spurts of energy, he started having seizures that made us feel helpless. The vet said he had several problems: mouth cancer, blindness, and heart disease. She gave us pills to administer several times a day. It took at least two of us to hold Skunk, and one would come away scratched and bleeding.

We moved once more, in February of 1992, to New Jersey. It was a three-hour drive to our new home. Skunk vomited three times on the way down and grumbled the entire trip. When we arrived, my adult son carried our cat around the fenced-in backyard, telling Skunk those were his boundaries.

Skunk deteriorated over the next sixteen months, growing thin and feeble. Every night he went down to my son's room and slept on a folded beach towel, leaving an imprint. One day in June of 1993 he just lay down and didn't move for hours. A friend came over to sit with me until the end. When I picked up his lifeless body to wrap in a towel, a last breath escaped. My son came home from work that evening and cried his eyes out. He found a box for Skunk, and we buried him under a tree in the backyard. There is still a circle of rocks at his grave with a small metal sign that reads: "Skunk Crossing." The beach towel with Skunk's imprint on it remained undisturbed until my son moved away.

Our daughter had stayed in Massachusetts, and our son moved to West Virginia a few months after Skunk died. My husband and I were on our own, truly empty-nesters. We hadn't thought about getting another pet; having just lost our seventeen-year-old cat, it did not seem like the right time. One day in December of 1993, however, we were strolling through a strip mall and came upon a cat adoption event.

I suggested we take a look; he said no. Next thing you know we're looking at this little ball of fluff with big green eyes staring back at us. Absolutely adorable! Her cage was labeled "Aspen," and she wore the colors of autumn leaves. A lady told us she was two years old and her owner was unable to care for her. Twenty minutes later, we were showing our new cat around the house.

We didn't like the name "Aspen"; it sounded pretentious, too cute. So we tried out some names, but nothing seemed to fit. I thought my late grandmother would love this cat as she looked a lot like her Toby. Light bulb went on! We named her Grace, after my grandmother. She also became Grace the Cat and, mostly, Gracie.

She was very timid and hid in the basement for weeks. Her litter box and food and water were down there, of course, but we wondered if Grace would ever come upstairs. We brought her up every day, but as soon as we put her down she headed for the basement. She was eating and using the litter box, but her tail lost all its hair and looked as if it belonged on a rat.

One afternoon I was sitting in a recliner in the living room when I saw movement out of the corner of my eye. I turned to look and there was Grace; she had finally come upstairs on her own. Not wanting to frighten her, I sat still and talked to her, saying her name. She jumped onto the raised footrest of my chair, made a small sound, curled up, and went to sleep.

Every time I was in that chair Grace would jump onto the footrest and sleep. Once in a while she would curl up on my chest, right under my chin, and purr softly. At night, she would follow us back to the bedroom and jump onto the bed. After we had settled in, she would sit next to my husband's face and pat him gently with her little paw. After an amount of time determined by only Grace, she would stretch out and go to sleep.

Grace had been declawed so there was no question she would be an indoor cat. She did escape several times, never went far, and would usually end up hiding under the deck. One summer day we saw her walking on the deck and were stumped as to how she had gotten out. We coaxed her back into the house, making sure the door was tightly closed. Several minutes later—there she was again, sitting on the deck railing. Again, we brought her in. We checked everywhere, found nothing amiss. It happened again; this time she was sitting atop the built-in air conditioner meowing. We collected her once more. A more thorough search revealed a window screen in the back of the house had fallen out. It was behind a curtain and never suspected as her point of egress. Determined to be free, Grace had discovered it and fooled us thrice.

Another day I was late for an appointment and rushing to leave. I did not see her before I left. It was a chilly day, but sunny. When I returned home three hours later, I found her plastered against the sliding doors to the deck—on the outside. She was very glad to see me open the doors but gave me a talking to as if it were my fault. We never knew how she had gotten out that day.

In 1996 we adopted our daughter's dog. He was a beautiful Rottweiler named Max. Gentle as a bunny, always ready to please, loved walks and ear rubs and butt scratches. When he first arrived, he and Grace warily checked each other out. If Max sniffed at her or got too close, she smacked him on the nose. He backed off every time. Grace became the "alpha" pet, although I believe Max allowed that because he liked her company. They lay side by side on the rug sharing the afternoon sunshine, and Grace would curl up next to him for naps.

Grace and Max were friends for ten years. Every evening at bedtime I would get up, get Max his three cookies and Grace her treat, and they would both head down the hall to the bedroom. Grace in the lead, Max behind, both making sure I was following. Grace would jump onto the bed, go to the middle to await my husband while Max sat by my nightstand to get his treats. This became our nightly routine without fail.

Max grew very ill and was put to sleep in August of 2006. Grace looked for him after he was gone. She developed diabetes soon after and was given insulin shots to the end of her life. Respiratory problems ensued, and the decision was made. Wrapped in a blanket, I held her as my husband drove to the vet one last time in the summer of 2008. Both Max and Grace were cremated, and their ashes sit one atop the other in my husband's office. We have been without a pet since, torn between enjoying their love and experiencing the inevitable sense of loss and pain when they cross the Rainbow Bridge.

Ty Alexander

By Stephanie Zelonis

When I was moving away to college, my mom decided that she would volunteer at a local cat shelter to keep herself busy. After volunteering for a few years, she met an orange Domestic Short-Haired cat named Ty. Ty was originally brought to the shelter by a lady who found him outside her home, begging for food. When he did not want to eat the wet food she gave him, she assumed he was sick and called the shelter for assistance. On the contrary, it turns out he only liked dry food, hinting that he had a former life in someone's home.

At the cat shelter, Ty got himself into a great deal of trouble, but my mom took a great liking to him. The volunteers kept the dry food stored in a large plastic container with a lid. Ty learned how to open the container and stick his head in, and you'd only be able to see his hind legs sticking out when he did this. The shelter ended up having to get a lock for the dry food container because he began teaching the other cats how to obtain the food! Additionally, whenever there was any type of altercation between the other cats, Ty was always the first one to run and see what was happening. He was very nosey, indeed! Unfortunately, Ty would often get "excited" and bite the volunteers. After he did this, as a precaution, he would have to go into the "quarantine cage" for nine lonely days. This was not a punishment; instead, it was time to make sure neither one became sick. After the nine days were over, he generally would re-bite someone, and the whole process would start over again!

After several months at the shelter, my mom learned that a family had adopted Ty. It seemed as though his luck was changing! Nine months later, when my mom walked into the shelter, the lead volunteer told her there was a surprise. She saw a cage with a sign that read "I'm back!" and Ty was inside. As it turns out, the family returned Ty because it "was not working out." How horrible for him to once again be uprooted from his surroundings!

At this point, my mom decided that she was interested in adopting Ty. Our family had always had cats, but did not currently have any. After about two months of deliberation, Ty became a member of our family. The adoption specialist at the shelter even offered to waive the adoption fee of $75 since my mom was a volunteer, but we still joke that maybe they were just glad to unload Ty from their facility!

Once in our home, we discussed whether or not we would rename Ty. We had heard conflicting views from others on this topic. Some people suggested we keep his name the same since that was what he was used to. Others said that a new start deserved a new name. After the help of a "baby name" book, I decided to add Alexander as a middle name to his existing name.

In our home, Ty Alexander is extremely spoiled and relishes in regal treatment daily. Every year on his birthday (which was appointed to him since the exact date is unknown), he gets a birthday balloon with his (approximate) age on it! He has countless beds and boxes around the house, which are lined with fleece that my mom purchases when she is out of state at one of her favorite stores. Ty Alexander even has his own chair at our kitchen table for when he joins us for meals (which is regularly). He wants undivided attention and always has to be on someone's lap. He thinks we can always sit with him, even at inconvenient times!

Since adopting Ty Alexander, we have also adopted an older, sixteen-year-old cat named Buddy and three kittens named Elizabeth, Patches, and April, who were born to a feral mother on our front porch (who are now almost three). Sometimes the kittens, who are younger than Ty Alexander and the newcomers to the house, swat at him or take his favorite chair. Despite being at our house longer, he is a gentleman and does not fight back. If they are in one of his favorite spots, he will simply find somewhere else to go. He really does not have competition, though—he is the favorite and always makes sure he is front and center in our lives.

Every day we are so thankful that Ty Alexander is a part of our family. Although the first few years of his life were not the easiest, he has been on "Cloud 9" in our home for over four years. He has finally found his true forever home and we couldn't be happier!

What About Me?

By Lucy (a.k.a. Anne Rollins)

Because I have beautiful golden eyes, my first mommy named me Topaz; but when my new mother took me in fourteen years ago, she called me Lucy Goosey. I'm glad she shortened it to Lucy because I was embarrassed to answer to Lucy Goosey in front of neighbors. I moved in with Mommy in January of 1990 after her precious Princess, a Himalayan, went to Cat Heaven. She's not a bad sort, my old fat mommy, and being her baby is rewarding. She lets me lick her dinner plate most of the time and feeds me American cheese, vanilla ice cream, and potato chips when she buys them. I get cow's milk, too, and that's okay because I'm a mature cat.

She talks to me in the third person—you know, "Mommy's gonna feed you now, Lucy." "Come to the kitchen with Mommy" or "Mommy loves you, Lucy." Gooey stuff like that. I give her kisses once a day. That way she thinks I love her, and I get more treats.

I'm a tortoiseshell cat—a "tortie" for short. Torties, compared to really low-class alley cats, are not recognized by cat fanciers so I'm not allowed to enter cat shows, which is very insulting to me. Mommy says I'm pretty. Or is she just saying that? Hmm.

I love to sit on Mommy's lap. She is soft like a pillow. But she screeches when I knead my paws into her thighs. How annoying that is! I like it even better when she lets me sit on her big fat chest. But she only seems to let me sleep on her chest when there's snow on the ground or it's cold out. Is she trying to tell me something? Sometimes when I do relax on her chest, she sneezes a lot, which is maddening.

This morning she didn't wake up when I nudged her with my paw. I walked back and forth over her body and heard her groan. Then I swatted her in the face. That works all the time. After all, it was five o'clock—time to get up and let me out! When I head down the long hallway, I can hear her muttering, "OUT! Lucy." I pretend to head for the door, but then I veer off and go for the kitchen. Another growl from her! She stands there leaning on her cane, her hair all messy, looking like she's still sleeping while I eat the cold food that she takes from the fridge. I'm sure she goes back to bed after I leave instead of cleaning my litter box and doing other cat chores. Or else, she's gone to that darn computer. I hate her computer, and someday I'll uninstall all her programs so that I can sit on her lap whenever I'm in the house. She pays no attention to me, and her office is such a mess!

I love the summer, and most every night I sleep outdoors under the stars. I know my mommy worries too much about me. At bedtime I always hear the "pssst" sounds she makes at the front door, but I make-believe I'm not around or don't hear her. Then I know she opens the living room window and psssts there. She's probably annoying my neighbors. If I feel like coming in, I do. Otherwise, I stay out all night. Speaking of sleeping outdoors all night, her handyman is driving me nuts. He works around Mommy's place, keeping things looking good. When Mommy asked him to cut down the ivy growing on the hu-mongous tree in the backyard, he also cut the bottoms of the young fir trees that I sleep between so now I'm exposed to all sorts of ferocious animals. I see the same possum walking by—sometimes with her babies trailing behind her—but she ignores me and keeps walking back to her home in the hot house. Once in a while I see a wild-eyed raccoon, but I stay away from that character. He's got big sharp talons and a nasty temper.

Mommy doesn't seem to have much to do this year. Last year it was fun because she had a lot of men coming in and out of her dining room. So I got lots of petting from them. Talk, talk, talk went on all day long. Most of her visitors like me and pet me all the time—except one guy who comes once a month to roundtable meetings in MY dining room. When I jump onto the dining room table and walk around so that everyone can pet me, he picks me up with one hand under my stomach and deposits me on the floor. What nerve! He's in MY HOUSE! But the other nice men make up for his hateful behavior, so I don't complain too much.

I want to tell you about this thing that Mommy sticks down my throat every day. It's a long stick filled with foul-tasting liquid that the doctor assured her I'd like. How does he know what I like or don't like? When she pleads to stick it in my mouth, I clamp my gums together and stare into her face. Doc's been sticking me in the neck with pins and needles, and I deliberately grit my gums and act like it doesn't hurt. But, I feel like screaming and scratching him. At last someone's noticed that I've been losing teeth and that I'm not the young pussycat I once was. They're trying to make me older than what I really am. First, they thought I was twelve, thirteen, or fourteen. Now they think I'm maybe nineteen or twenty. They could have asked me—but I'm not telling. I have been eating my mother out of cat food and that's because I've developed something that sounds like "hyperthyroidism."

119

In other words, overactive thyroid. That's why I have a slim figure. Too bad my mommy doesn't get a little hyper-something-or-other. Don't get me wrong! I don't want mommy to be sick. But she should lose a little weight so that I don't lose HER.

Did I mention the two annoying felines that invade MY territory? One is a black and white male named Thomas who used to live next door. When his mistress moved to another state, she didn't take him with her, so he is living nearby with a new person named Nancy. Well, Thomas still comes over to MY territory and sleeps on MY front steps. My mommy thinks I don't know it, but she brings him in MY house when I'm not around because I can smell him. I know he plays with MY toys and eats MY food! On top of that, he tries to attack me. Ingrate! Then there's this small white and black female named Lulu who lives across the way from me. I don't go near her, but she screams at the top of her lungs and hisses at me even when I mind my own business. So, she asks for it and I give it. I chase her through the grove of trees, and she's all the time screaming. Then she hides in a secret place, one that my mother isn't aware of and will remain a secret. Mommy even lets her come in MY house once in a while. I don't like any of this. I don't go in their homes and I think they should stay out of mine.

One time when I first moved in, I brought my mommy a present—a cute baby squirrel that I took from its nest in a tall tree. The darn thing kept wiggling and shivering and making squeaky sounds. I carried it through the screen in the window that I had ripped open and my mother didn't appreciate that. She hit me with the broom and brought the baby squirrel back out to the grove of trees. I watched while she guessed which tree I had taken the baby from, but I wouldn't let on.

I love it when Mommy combs my fur, but I hate it when she tries to put the flea and tick medicine on my neck. She wears these thick yellow rubber gloves to protect herself from the chemicals. Yet she doesn't worry about what the chemicals will do to me. It may keep the fleas and ticks away, but what about me? But she makes me feel not so ugly and strokes me a lot.

When I'm sitting on my mother's lap while she watches television, I sometimes hear her crying. She cries at anything that's beautiful or sad or even happy. She's a complex woman, this mother of mine. One big problem, though, that I worry about—I sometimes hear her saying that if anything bad happens to her, she doesn't want me to become homeless again and wants me put to sleep. Well, hey baby, she may be going to sleep, but that doesn't mean I should be put to sleep. But then, my mommy wants only for me to be happy, and I wouldn't be happy without her lap or chest to sit on and all the "I love yous" I get from her. Yes, can't you tell that I really do love my mommy? That's why I allow her to live in MY house!

Beasle, the Unforgettable Cat

By Cheryl DeVleeschouwer

I never knew how heartbroken I would feel when my firstborn son left for college.

For weeks my tears flowed whenever I thought of him or walked past his empty bedroom. I prayed to God to give me strength and help ease the loss.

Within a couple of weeks, a miracle happened. A feral black kitten, about three months old, showed up in our back woods. After multiple attempts to catch him, it was only when I bought a live trap cage that we succeeded.

His fur was jet black, and he had the most beautiful yellow/green eyes. His two side teeth hit his lower lip and looked like fangs. I knew that he was here for a reason, and I was determined to tame him.

We named him Beasle and kept him in a huge cage at the end of our hallway. Every day, I would sit at the other end of the hall, and just talk to him. As the days passed, I moved a little closer to him. Eventually, he licked the milk off of my fingers.

And then magic happened. After two weeks, he walked out of his cage and laid on his back. Carefully, I moved closer and slowly put my hand out. He started to roll back and forth. Gently, I rubbed his belly and he started to purr. Tears were rolling down my face. He was mine, and I was his.

After that miraculous day, he became the sweetest and most perfect cat. He loved to sleep in my plants—I think that reminded him of his days living in the woods. He loved to help me make my bed. In fact, I would sometimes try to sneak upstairs so he would not follow me.

That never worked. He always found me. He loved to get under the sheet and then attack me as I was trying to put the top sheet on. How I wish I had one more day to play with him like that.

When the weather was warm, he would cry at the door to go outside. I tried to ignore his pleas, but his meows only got louder. He was missing the woods and running free. With much hesitation, I opened the door and let him out. He started running as fast as he could right into our woods. My heart was sad but I knew I had to let him go. I watched him until he ran out of sight, thinking I may never see him again. About an hour later, I decided to go outside and call him to see if he would come back. No luck the first time. The second time, I called him and clapped my hands. Within seconds, he came charging out of the woods and right to me.

He rubbed against my legs and let me pick him up. He was home, and I was beyond happy. That became our thing—he meowed at the door, I let him out for a while and whenever I clapped my hands and called him, he always came running back.

Beasle loved our dog, Pepper, and our cat, Cuddles, and they all became best friends. Every evening, when we sat down in the family room the action began. Beasle would chase Pepper and tackle him, and together they would roll on the floor. It was a chase and catch game between the two of them until they exhausted themselves. The two of them would cuddle together in the dog's bed. Cuddles would sit beside them wanting to be part of the gang.

Beasle was a friend to everyone he met. When the doorbell rang, he was the first one to run to the door to greet our guests. No matter who came to visit, Beasle always jumped on their laps and wanted to be part of the action. He became known as the friendliest cat in the neighborhood.

One day, a mouse was running around in our family room. Beasle was sitting in the middle of the floor just watching the mouse scurry about. He seemed to have more pleasure watching me scramble to catch it than do it himself. Mice were not his thing. We were not sure if Beasle thought he was a dog or a person.

The years passed, and Beasle was the most loving and awesome cat. He showed us how remarkably smart and caring he was. One early morning, around four a.m., I heard strange sounds coming from downstairs. When I went to the kitchen, I found Pepper having seizures on the floor. Beasle and Cuddles were right there beside him. Those cats never left his side even after I tried to send them away.

After losing our dog, it was a very quiet house. We witnessed the sadness felt by Beasle and Cuddles. They did not play or run around. They were mourning the loss of their best friend.

Fortunately, time heals and before we knew it, the cats were back to their playful fun-loving selves. For sixteen years, we were blessed to have these bundles of joy in our lives.

Two years ago, we noticed Beasle was losing weight and did not want to go outside. The vet confirmed his kidneys were failing and there was nothing that could be done. We brought him home and decided to give him the best care and lots of love.

Our final visit to the vet was one of the saddest days of my life. The tears would not stop flowing. We held him and told him how much we loved him and thanked him for all the wonderful memories. He put his little face up to mine and peacefully fell asleep for the last time.

We are so grateful that Beasle came into our lives. He is and will always be my unforgettable cat.

Jay-Jay, the Cat Who Rescued Me

By Rosemary DeTrolio

My husband and I wanted a cat after we lost a beloved pet. We decided to adopt a kitten. The very next day, my husband was working at the Jenny Jump State Forest when a loud kitten came out of safety and cried out to him. This beautiful tabby was so insistent, he realized she was trying to save herself and two little sisters from starvation. He scooped her up and the other two little kittens followed.

He took all three home to live with us, but we bonded with Jay Jay, the brave little kitty who saved her family.

She quickly acclimated to our home life. When she was a kitten, she'd make up games, dropping a scrap of paper from the top of a chair and then racing off the chair to catch the paper before it fluttered to the ground. Jay-Jay was fearless. She decided to make friends with the seventy-five-pound Golden Retriever, daring to pet the dog under its chin through a safety gate.

Each night, she slept under my neck and cuddled with me.

Jay-Jay brought me through the death of my Golden Retriever, and later, the death of my beloved father and mother. She stroked my hair and comforted me. She had a knack of knowing who needed her.

Once we lost our Golden, we got a Cockapoo and tried a prayer of intention. A scrappy eleven-pound Shih-Tzu emerged from the woods, half-dead and nursing a three-pound pug dog. We adopted her, too, and found a home for the pug. Once we had all the pets at home, the Shih-Tzu had a scuffle with Jay-Jay. We didn't know the cause. We soon realized that Jay-Jay had been sneaking the dog's food and the Shih-Tzu saw her do it.

Jay-Jay was a stunning cat in her "teen years" and spoke fluent "dog." She'd roll on her belly so people could pet her, and she'd growl at the dogs if they bothered her. She never once raised a paw to hurt either of them.

In later years, Jay-Jay ballooned into a fluffy twenty-three pounds of love. She enjoyed food, and her huge body was a testament to her appetite and dog-food stealing activities.

Today, my beautiful sweet cat crossed the Rainbow Bridge, and I cried a bucket of tears. She will always have a place in my heart, and I'll never forget the love she brought when she rescued me.

Sugar

By Shelby Nelson

As I stood at the SAVE animal shelter in Princeton, NJ, I instantly fell in love with a small gray and white kitten with a pink nose and huge paws. She is a polydactyl cat, having six toes on both of her front paws. Since she wasn't quite four weeks old, I was unable to take her home at the time. I waited anxiously for the call that she was ready for me to pick her up. Upon picking her up, I named her Sugar since she was so sweet.

I have had many cats in the past and knew instantly that Sugar was a very intelligent, intuitive cat. From the very beginning, she understood my moods and was very comforting whenever I was under the weather.

Several years later, I fell in love with the man who would later become my husband. His name is Carl. Sugar fell in love with Carl also. One summer, he had hurt his back and was unable to work. She would lie with him every day. Out of nowhere, she began to knead him with her big paws all over his abdominal area for very long periods of time. He then began to have some stomach issues. It was as if she sensed that something was going on in there. This went on for at least a week. She was genuinely concerned about him, and you could tell she just wanted him to feel better.

I took Carl to the doctor, and they found the issue that was causing the discomfort. They gave him medication and told him it would take about twenty-four hours to take care of the problem. When I brought him home, Sugar gave him one of her cat massages, and they both fell asleep together.

The next morning, Carl was feeling much better. Sugar jumped up on him and started to give him his daily massage. After a few seconds, she stopped and put her ear to his stomach to listen. She knew that he was feeling better. She patted him twice on the shoulder with her paw, gave him a kiss with her pink nose, and walked away.

Her job was done! He was all better. From that day on, we have called her Doctor Sugar. Whenever either of us has any kind of ailment, she is right there taking care of us.

The Unseen Hand

By Wendy Hanek

I've always been intrigued by the phrase "everything happens for a reason." If that were a true statement, perhaps this unpredictable life would make more sense. My father-in-law used to talk about the "unseen hand" guiding people through life, and this got me thinking of the idea of fate even more but never did I start believing in it until I met my cat Wilson. Looking back at all the random twists in this little guy's young life and how our paths crossed made me a believer.

Most would think that Furgus, our large orange tomcat with the surly face and determined eyes would be enough to handle. He had the habit of waking me up at five a.m., the audacity to sneak cold cuts out of sandwiches when his victim was unsuspecting, and the nerve to nip family members on the bottom when his meals were not served promptly. I found myself looking over my shoulder to make sure I was not going to be attacked while preparing meals, although I was usually so sleep deprived that I barely noticed when Furgus would sneak up on me. A cat "expert" at work suggested that a friend was just what he would need. Apparently, if he had another feline to play with, these pushy behaviors would stop. Although my husband and I talked over the idea of getting another cat, we were not convinced that it would help with his behavior. "Furgus is just Furgus, and he probably won't change his ways," my husband would insist.

Nonetheless, we decided to check out the New Jersey Cat Show in Somerset since they were supposed to host many animal rescue organizations. The weekend of the show was a hectic one for my family since it was filled with tennis lessons and ice hockey games. Although we planned to get there on Saturday, the first day of the show, we could not fit it in between activities. When we were not able to make it, I imagined that the most sociable cats were probably long gone and that the feral ones would be waiting for us when we arrived the next day.

On the day of the show, my family was slow to get ready but we made it within the last few hours. By that time, I was downtrodden since I expected most of the cats to be gone. As we made our way through the parking lot, I was filled with anticipation. Would I find a friend for Furgus? As I opened the door to the convention hall, I was astonished to behold a sea of cats all lined up in cages and crowds of people flocked around them.

Through all the commotion, I saw two very large ears poking up at the top of a cage on the far side of the convention center. I'm still not sure how, but the "unseen hand" guided me past all the other cages and straight to Wilson. Along the way I didn't stop to look at any other cat. Wilson was the only one in my trajectory. As we approached, he started to perk up, and when we were before him, I noticed that he was proudly sporting a bowtie in an effort to impress prospective adopters. He was the most beautiful buff and white cat I have ever seen with wide yellow eyes and milky white fir with some buff flairs. As soon as we stood in front of the cage, he flipped on his back, extended his arm, and touched me. At that moment, he also touched my heart and I knew he was the one, not just for Furgus, but for me.

Suddenly my heart sank when I noticed that unlike the rest of the cats from this shelter who had tags displayed on their cages, his was gone. Had he already found a home? It felt like an eternity before one of the volunteers came over. "Are you interested?" she flatly asked as she probably asked so many others that weekend. "Is he still available?" I asked quickly as if hurrying my words would make a difference. "Are we too late? "You're just on time actually," she said. "Wilson just made it out of quarantine and just got here a little while ago. We quarantine cats when they just come in to make sure they are healthy before exposing them to other cats. He's quite healthy but he's lucky to be alive." She went on to explain that he had been attacked by a pack of feral cats when he was on the streets. He screamed so loud that a woman in a nearby house heard, opened her door, and was shocked to see a little, beat-up cat run in. It just so happened that this woman ran the shelter. Wilson definitely picked the right house! And we picked the right cat.

As I stand in the kitchen at five a.m. preparing my children's lunches in the morning, guarding the cold cuts from my insatiable tomcat while simultaneously getting nipped in the rear, I often forget that the reason we got Wilson was to distract Furgus and to detract from his assertive behaviors. I know that fate led us to Wilson because he fits perfectly into our family. Furgus is still Furgus, but he is so much happier having a little buddy to look after...and so are we.

Cat Bed Project

By Walter O'Brien

A seven-year-old township girl was so determined to bring comfort to as many shelter cats as possible, she has sewn 60 cat beds on her own sewing machine to donate to local cat shelters.

Ava Vallely, who has three cats of her own – Johnny, Jack and Violet – got her inspiration from a visit to a cat sanctuary in Ringoes, New Jersey, which has rescued hundreds of cats in hopeless situations of all kinds since about 2003. The facility holds nearly 100 cats at any one time and features adoption services, a hopsital and hospice care.

The visit was arranged through PAWS for Reading, a program that allows children to read aloud to therapy dogs, cats or even bunnies, in order to improve the children's reading and communication skills.

Ava decided to go on a mission to help the many cats in need at Tabby's Place, as well as the animal welfare center in the North Branch section of Branchburg, by crafting her own cat beds, according to her parents, Roseanne and Joe Vallely.

Ava created the charity name, "Pads-4-Purrs," did some fundraising on her own, and used her tooth fairy money to begin sewing the cat beds on her new sewing machine.

She's collected fabric and money from friends to buy more supplies.

So far she has sewn 60 pet beds and is looking forward to delivering them to the shelters in April.

Her goal is to buy more fabric, fiber-fill and thread to make more beds. She'd also like to collect money to donate towards pet food as well so she can donate that to the shelters along with her beds.

"We are very proud of Ava's dedication and concern for those in need," her mother, Roseanne Vallely, said. "This has been a big labor of love for her and we're glad she saw it to fruition."

"I am a third grade teacher at Martin Luther King Jr. Elementary School in Edison, and have always encouraged my kids (students and my own) to realize that their size doesn't limit their reach," Roseanne said. "Ava has always said, 'Mommy, I'm small but I can do big things!' Words to a mother's ears!"

Ava is looking ahead to make her next batch of 30 beds, along with food and treats packages, by the end of the school year or early summer. She hopes to collect more donations and to enlist the help of her friends through sewing session play-dates. She hopes that "Pads-4-Purrs" will inspire other kids to do the same in their own towns.

Originally published in the **Hunterdon Review** as
7-year-old Clinton Twp. girl sews 60 beds for shelter cats

Jaeger and Bello: Ambassadors of Hope

By Angela Hartley

Sometimes it seems like this old world's tree is being shaken down to its roots.

Nepal. Baltimore. Yemen. Leaves scattered to the four winds.

When the foundations are crumbling, what can the righteous do? Borrow the gaze of smaller, sager creatures.

Weeks like these, we feel very small.

We can donate to The American Red Cross®. We can pray for peace. We can plant small saplings of love and justice in our daily dealings. These are small things that aren't small.

But in the dark and the quiet, we ache with all the aches of the earth. We're all in this together—and that's a good thing, but it also means that if one part hurts, we all hurt.

The American Red Cross® is a registered trademark of The American National Red Cross.

135

If we ever needed the soothing grace of a Great Soul, it would be now.

And God provides.

Jaeger and Bello came to Tabby's Place® with no great fanfare. Two older cats, bereaved and bereft and blown off by extended family, found their way to us. Standard story. Nothing newsworthy.

Nothing...but everything.

Big and blundering, Bello was a love-whirl who instantly deserved the same name as the Ringling Bros®. clown. He bombles about in Suite C, klutzing towards humans and lumbering towards cats. He is a big, lovey burbler, twelve years old and ten trillion laughs young.

Bello is making us laugh.

But if Bello is the fool (in the positive, Shakespearean sense — think Touchstone or Puck, not Adam Sandler), Jaeger is the priestess.

She doesn't have the moves like Jagger. Her hazel-brownie-amber eyes can scarcely make out shadows. But if you're looking for a more blissful buzz and lasting lift than the finest Jägermeister can deliver, look to the long loaf of tabby in the Community Room.

Really, the Community Room. Jaeger was intended (by us real fools) to be a Lobby cat. But Jaeger knew from the git-go that she had

Tabby's Place: a Cat Sanctuary is a service mark of Tabby's Place: a Cat Sanctuary, Inc.

Ringling Brothers is a registered trademark of Ringling Bros. — Barnum & Bailey Combined Shows, Inc.

a higher purpose. The nature of her calling? Healing humanity, one soul at a time.

So it was a soft-pawed slide into the Community Room. Since she moved in, Jaeger hasn't stopped resting her velvet feet in our laps:

"Prithee thee, may I give you A Love?"

If you say no, the lady doth protest just enough. Taptap. Paw-paw-pawpawpaw. Soft. Subtle. But certain.

"Verily, blithe soul, thou art in need of A Love. Pardon me to bestow at least a Half-Cuddle?"

And you art in need. Verily. So you scoot back in your chair, and, ladylike, Jaeger vaults into your lap.

And now you're not going anywhere for a very, very long time.

Neither are you worrying, despairing, or diving face-first into all the angst that assaults you. You're suddenly, startlingly consumed by those hazel-brownie-amber eyes.

It's a quiet thing, a radiant thing, Jaeger's liturgy of love. Our striped, sightless mistress of divinity will walk small circles in your lap before settling herself into a purr-puddle. For reasons known only to Jaeger and God, the old tabby will "look" at you—right in the eyes, no less—the whole time.

Medicine tells us that Jaeger's eyes barely see. But Jaeger herself sees. Spend enough time in her presence, and you'll see it, too: grace.

Healing.

A hope and a future.

Just like the mystery hitting Jaeger's old retinas, we don't know quite what that looks like. But we know, beyond the last sliver of sunset, that it's real.

And until faith becomes sight and the healing is whole, we've got ministering spirits in tabby stripes.

Originally published in 2015, *Ambassadors of Hope*
is reprinted with permission from Tabby's Place,
a cat sanctuary in Ringoes, New Jersey. www.tabbysplace.org

B.W.'s Tale

By Karen and Bruce Gray

I've decided to start our family's story of rescuing pets with B.W. He wasn't our first pet, but his story shows our commitment to helping animals and the love he returned in gratitude for helping him.

My husband Bruce and I first spotted B.W. on a visit to my aunt's house in Brooklyn. My Aunt Helen's story of rescuing pets could be the topic of another book. She had many cats and with her limited funds took good care of them.

Lounging in Aunt Helen's front yard was the handsomest black and white young cat I'd ever seen. He had a lot more white than a typical tuxedo cat. He seemed about six months old, no longer a kitten, but clearly not full grown. We had adopted a dog in 1989, and we hadn't thought about additional pets. Our dog, Misty was adopted from a rescue group. Based on a lot of reading I'd done, and understanding of the huge animal overpopulation problem in the U.S., it was clearly the way to go. I guess at that moment, I put this young cat in the back of my mind to discuss adopting him with Bruce later. Since my aunt had so many cats in her house, I could not expect her to take in more. And I knew we could provide a good home for him.

It was probably September or October of 1993. By December, we were ready to make our move. We were planning to visit Aunt Helen and asked her to try to get this cute guy into a carrying case for us to take him home. I wasn't optimistic, because outdoor cats can be fearful and I thought it might take several tries to catch him.

We arrived and my aunt said he was in the carrying case. I was surprised, but thrilled, of course! Young B.W. would be moving to New Jersey. That is what I had decided to name him. Bruce thought I wanted to name him "Black and White", but B.W. worked for me. Little did I realize that almost 20 years later, lots of people would be known by their initials, like a favorite Mets pitcher of mine.

On the way home, we learned something about B.W. that would be a concern about him for many years to come. He got incredibly car sick. On this trip he may have just vomited, but in the future, we would learn that he got so nervous, he often did every bodily function in his carrying case. Two things ended up helping with this situation, a carrying case with both a side and top opening, and eventually some medication suggested by one of the wonderful vets who cared for B.W. during his life.

So B.W. arrived in New Jersey, and quickly adapted well to his new life. This brings up one of the mysteries of B.W's life Over the years, I would come to learn much about feral cats and kittens. Clearly B.W. was not a typical cat born on the streets that was fearful of people. He loved everyone not just us! Of all our cats, he was one that never hid from visitors, was friendly and outgoing. So we thought B.W. was probably not born as a stray or if he was, he may have been taken into a house early in his life, and later ran off or was abandoned. Possibly someone knew my aunt cared for cats and put him in her front yard. We will never know, but our young man was not afraid of people, in fact, he sought people out to befriend and purr for them.

We of course had him examined by our vet, and neutered. He got car sick on the way to the vet, and even though we eventually figured out some solutions to that problem, the greatest solution towards the end of his life was to use a mobile vet. He enjoyed being in Dr. De-Maria's mobile vet hospital, because of course he was not afraid of his vet's, it was just the ride getting there that upset him.

B.W.'s first vet did notice his front legs were stiff. Although no vet ever really focused on it as a major physical problem, it did make him look like he was stomping around the house, maybe just a tad bit angry looking. We knew he wasn't angry though, he was the happiest cat ever.

B.W. actually led a lot of uneventful years. He came to share his house with many other pets. He and Misty the dog were the only two until 1996. We then adopted another cat, who B.W. really didn't interact with much for many years, because we were afraid they wouldn't get along and given the layout of our house in two distinct levels, we let B.W. be Mr. Upstairs and Yankee was Mr. Downstairs. Misty was an only dog for years until we found Hobo. So, B.W. had one cat brother and two dog sisters. He got along with everyone and they all got along with him. So it was the two cats for many years until 2002, when we became aware of the many stray/feral cats in our neighborhood. So from then on, many cats have entered our doors, all strays, all accepted by the existing pets and all loved immensely. B.W. was friendly to all, but you know, we always thought he thought of himself more of a dog, acting more like a dog, and hanging out with the dogs more than the other cats.

Eventually B.W. started having a lot of loose bowel movements. We have come to learn that many vets treat the symptoms and don't try to find out what the problem is. So he was treated with some meds for a while, but we realized that he wasn't really improving and maybe he should get some more attention. We actually sought out a vet we had been using at one practice who had moved to a different practice. We took B.W. in the car almost an hour to see this vet, who suggested he have an ultrasound at her office the following week or so. We brought him there, and had a huge disappointment in terms of getting good advice from a vet. The person who came to the vet's office and did the ultrasound was incredibly late, which wouldn't have bothered us that much if we had received good news, but after the ultrasound was over, the vet came into the waiting room and told us B.W. had cancer, and I hate to say this, suggested we get ready to say our good-byes to him.

Well, I've become a fighter for those I love, and I was going to fight hard to save the life of my 13-year-old cat. The vet mumbled something about taking him to a holistic vet practice, which we chose to do. We scheduled an appointment with Dr. Gloria Binkowski, one the of nicest, most compassionate smart people we have ever met. She suggested we take B.W. to see on oncologist. Which is of course what we did. We were going to fight to help our brave, car sick boy!

The oncologist was in Red Bank, NJ. I think it was then we got some medication for B.W. to help with the car ride, which was a little bit over one hour. Dr. Clifford examined B.W., and he was one of many vets that noticed it was very hard to hear his heart beat, his purring was so loud. B.W. would have to have surgery, and his growth would be removed and biopsied. No problem. Anything to get our boy well.

We had a lot of luck with our B.W. getting to Dr. Binkowksi who suggested going to Red Bank, and his becoming a patient of Dr. Clifford. His cancer turned out to be small cell lymphoma, a much less aggressive cancer. He would be on chemotherapy pills that we could administer ourselves with just an occasional visit to Dr. Clifford to check his progress.

B.W. did fantastic. He was very easy to pill—thanks to Pill Pockets™ which ended up being a huge help with many of our pets. We started giving him the pills every third day, then eventually even less often. Soon he was in remission. I know I did not will him to his cure, but I was so determined not to lose a 13-year-old cat to cancer, especially such a personable one. We were so lucky!

Things were going well for B.W. until the early fall of 2008. He was having some issues particularly not eating as well. We were watching him closely. We had a very good experience at the University of Pennsylvania with our new dog Saffron so we took B.W. on a two-hour ride to the emergency room at UPenn on a Sunday. B.W. had actually been there on a visit once before, but they really did not find anything critical in the previous visit. We were so impressed with the UPenn doctors we didn't think of taking him anywhere else.

Upon arrival BW was a very sick boy. His kidney values were through the roof. We would not be taking him home with us. Their goal was to try to get his values down, and the kidney specialists would see him in the morning.

I feel like I am doing a cliff hanger here, stalling with what happened with B.W., but I need to preach for a minute. All of this treat-

Pill Pockets are a trademark of the Nutro Company, Inc., a subsidiary of Mars, Inc.

ment for B.W. was expensive, even the Chemo pills, but you know what? Every penny we spent on B.W. was worth it. There was no price that could ever be put on the extra time we had with B.W. I know many people have very little savings. I know right now the economy is bad. But you know, some vet practices have CareCredit which allows you to pay your bills over time. Others will let you pay a portion every month. And to save their beloved pets, some people could actually eat out less often, or get one less manicure. These are your precious pets. Vets have student loans to pay back too. We would love it if vets could lower their prices to help us, but if you are willing to pay for that airfare to go on vacation, or for that new outfit, you can pay for your precious pet's vet care. We did.

So back to B.W. at UPenn. We found out that he needed surgery to put a stint in his kidney to allow his kidney to function. I was letting Bruce speak to the surgeon, I was way too nervous. Dr. Allyson Berent explained everything to Bruce, and said if the surgery didn't go well, he would not wake up, she would "put him to sleep". Well, it seemed like years until we heard from UPenn, but his surgery was over, and it went as well as could be expected. It was Tuesday. We would drive to Philadelphia on Saturday to see him, although he probably wouldn't be ready to come home. He held his own for those days, and the surgery appeared to have worked well.

He was still in rough shape from the surgery when we arrived for our visit on Saturday. He was in the ICU. The entire staff was shocked how when he saw us, he struggled to get up to greet us. It was a great visit. So great, we went back the next day on Sunday. I think he was tired on Sunday, but of course was still glad to see us. He stayed there in the ICU for over 10 days, and I think I was able to bring him home the following Thursday or Friday. He was not great when he was first home, and after several visits back to UPenn, he needed a second surgery for a bigger stint. Ultimately, his kidney surgery was successful, and we had our boy back again.

He needed subcutaneous fluids on a daily basis, which I think ultimately caused him another problem, but we gladly administered them and he was for the most part, cooperative. The only reason he would fuss and break away from us when giving the fluids was he was a busy boy, he needed to move and do things, so he didn't want to be hooked up to the bag of fluids for so long. Another side effect of this surgery was in 2009 he did develop a lump/growth at the IV site, and that growth was ultimately cancerous, but we did not lose B.W. to that.

Dr. Berent ended up leaving UPenn and coming to work in New York City. That should have been good for us, no more 2 hour trips to see her in Pa. However, during the transition, we did not have him examined other than by Dr. Clifford for his leg growth. I guess the year of fluids had done damage to his heart. When we finally saw Dr. Berent in NYC on Columbus Day 2009, she was concerned about his heart and we got him to a cardiologist. From the day of his first illness with the small cell lymphoma until now, it had been well over 3 years. I guess we were running out of luck. I always estimated B.W.'s birthdate to be March 1993. It was now November 2009. He was well over 16. Friends of ours had their two cats about 20 years. We were not going to be that lucky. B.W.'s heart disease was severe. No treatment could really help. We brought him home from the cardiologist hoping to give him some more quality time. We only got about a month from the appointment in the city with Dr. Berent. He was so bad, Dr. DeMaria came to the house and helped us end his suffering early on a Tuesday morning. As a college instructor, I really had to go to class

145

that day, and I did. Dr. DeMaria thought he was pretty bad off and might not have survived the day.

The bottom line is he was the most charming, friendly cat we ever met. The vet at the practice where the initial ultrasound was done told us to say our goodbyes, we wouldn't have him much longer. Some people might think he suffered with the kidney surgery. Why did we do it? In fact, we were told at UPenn, some of the students questioned why you would do surgery like that on a 15 year old cat. Why? Because he was B.W., and he enjoyed living. Each day was an adventure for him, fun and joyful. He charmed all he met. People who met him who weren't big fans of cats liked him. He had visitors during his recuperation. He was 'The Man' and always will be. We will never have another cat like him. Our cat, Dandy comes close, and his big personality fills the house, but we will never forget B.W. and his charm!

A Stable Hero: "Pole Cat"

By Jan Cross Cubbage

During Thanksgiving of 1977 I took a short break from my career as a jockey and spent several days with my family in New Jersey. After a pleasant stay with my folks I loaded up my yellow Buick Sky Hawk and hit the highway. Tampa, Florida was my destination.... actually a few miles west of Tampa to the area known as Oldsmar, where a thoroughbred race track called "Florida Downs" was located.

I made some genuine friends while practicing my craft as a jockey at Florida Downs. One Saturday evening, horse owners Cooper and Candy Barrett, invited me to their Tarpon Springs home for dinner, the first of many. Cooper was an architect and Candy created meals that played havoc with my weight-control efforts.

While enjoying yet another dinner at the Barrett's home near Christmas time, I noticed that their calico house cat was looking very close to having kittens. Sure enough, on New Year's Day I drove again to Cooper and Candy's home and found that the mama cat had five little kittens and was nesting with them in the guest room closet. By the end of February, Cooper and Candy were asking me which of the five kittens I wanted to adopt.

I was leaving Florida Downs at the end of March and intending to end my career as a jockey at that time. I had concrete plans to take on an assistant trainer's job with a stable, heading from Florida to Churchill Downs, home of the Kentucky Derby. I had never been to this race horse fan's classic event and was looking forward to living in Louisville for two months. I did not need or desire to own a cat. I did not even know where I was going to stay when I got to Louisville but I had already been advised that finding a place to live would be no easy task. When trying to lease an apartment during my rather vagabond lifestyle, I recalled the abundance of "NO PETS" signs encountered. On the other hand, how could I turn down a "gift" from the couple whom had practically adopted me during my winter season race riding days in Florida. So I picked out one of the colorful kittens. My new furry roommate turned out to be a very tough and incredibly smart feline friend throughout all of her nine lives and eighteen years.

I named her "Pole Cat," PC for short. I am of Polish descent, so my cat was dubbed a "Pole Cat." Like her mother, PC was a mix of blended colors and sported a white belly and chest, white paws and a head crowned with white-tipped ears. I still had a few weeks left at Florida Downs to ride, so I took my new roommate home and quite enjoyed her kitten antics and acrobatics. Little PC was afraid of nothing. I was staying at a small trailer park in the country and before long PC was attacking lizards and leaping at sparrows in her out-of-door adventures. PC and a red Chihuahua who lived next door became friends and chased each other around the yards surrounding our trailers.

148

At the end of March, my feline roommate and I were packed and driving to Louisville, Kentucky. PC sat on top of a box on the passenger's seat and scouted the scenery. During the trip north, I taught PC to walk on a leash. She did this quite willingly. There really was not any room in my over packed car for a litter box. So, I walked PC on a leash at roadside rest stops and she did her duty just as a dog would.

As soon as I arrived in Louisville I began my search for a place to stay. Just about a dozen blocks from the stable entrance of Churchill Downs I spotted a "Room For Rent" sign posted on the front lawn of a majestic Victorian era home, complete with gingerbread trim and a large cupola.

With anticipation and crossed fingers, I pulled into the driveway, parked and rang the doorbell. A trim, white haired lady opened the door and I inquired about the room. The lady informed me that it was a large upstairs room, where the cupola was located. But, the matron stated firmly that she "only leased rooms to gentlemen". While she was telling me this I peered into the interior of the house and spied three cats sprawled out on the lower steps of the stairway. Sensing that this elderly lady adored cats, I told the owner of the house that I had brought a kitten with me from Florida. Next thing I recall, the front door was opened wide and I was offered an invitation for afternoon tea. Ms. Mary Lou and I conversed about the upcoming Kentucky Derby favorites and felines. She had six cats in her home, all named after Kentucky Derby winners. By the time our teacups were empty I had a stately upstairs room secured for the race meet—all because I had brought PC with me!

Fast- forward two years to March of 1979 and I was the trainer of six horses at Gulfstream Park race track located in Hallandale, Florida, just north of Miami. Pole Cat had become a bona fide stable cat who sometimes came home with me to my apartment if I could sneak her in. Most of the time though PC was very content to stay at the stables, patrolling our shed row for mice, rats and pigeons. At six AM, upon my daily arrival at the stable, I would find PC stationed on the door mat in front of the tack room/office room door, watching over my string of race horses. My horses seemed to know that PC was some how in charge of law and order in the shed row. Prowling around the shed row and sometimes wandering into stalls, the horses nuzzled her and obviously enjoyed her company.

There was, however, that fierce side to PC. All trespassers were greeted with a loud growling whether they were human, or goat, or cat, or whatever. PC knew the hired riders and grooms, our vet and farrier, and all members of our racing team. PC communicated her friendship to all on a daily basis with her purring and leg rubbing. But, all others beware of the fiery orange, black, gray and white-footed stable cat that was apt to run you down and grab an ankle in her very sharp teeth. PC developed quite the reputation in the stable area of Gulfstream Park as my stable "guard cat."

At the end of the Gulfstream Park race meet, I made arrangements for my six horses to be shipped to Atlantic City race track, located near the New Jersey shore town of the same name. A trainer named Joe Hines was hauling a few of his own horses up to New Jersey and had room in his long, fifth-wheel trailer for my six. Joe usually had his twenty-one-year-old son ride with him, but unfortunately, Joe's son was battling cancer and could not make the trip. I was leaving about twelve hours before Joe and my horses so I could set up my stable and have stalls ready for my steeds when they arrived. A friend was loading my horses into Joe's trailer for me.

The evening of my departure for New Jersey, Joe spoke with me and he had an odd request. Joe asked me if I would leave Pole Cat with my horses and let her ride alongside him in his truck cab for the trip north. I was fairly amused by the request for I had no idea that this tall Florida cowboy had affections for my cat. I thought about it for a minute, for usually PC was my designated co-pilot on road trips. But, one look at Joe's face and I could sense that he really did need some one riding in his pickup's shot gun seat, even if it be a stable cat. So I took off for Atlantic City race track leaving my PC behind in Joe's care and hoped she would not be upset riding with Joe and not me.

The following is Joe's story of what happened on their journey north hauling nine race horses. Joe said he pulled out of the stable gate of Gulfstream Park with his rig and horses in the early morning and by late evening was nearing the North Carolina border. Joe stopped at a truck stop plaza near South of the Border, fueled his truck, provided water and hay to the horses, grabbed some coffee, walked Pole Cat on her leash and was then back on Interstate 95 heading north. Joe said he got some sideways looks from truck drivers as he walked "his cat" on a leash around the plaza but that he and PC were just getting along fine.

About twenty minutes into North Carolina, traffic moving along and making good time, PC suddenly took a fit. The PC that usually fell asleep or quietly watched the scenery go by became extremely agitated, howling loudly and pawing insistently at Joe's sleeve. Joe said he cussed her out a bit for he was fairly certain she was telling him that she had to make a pee or poop stop. And, they had only been back on the road for twenty minutes! But, Joe pulled his rig off the interstate at the next exit and steered into a gas station parking lot. As soon as Joe opened his truck's door and his boots hit the pavement

151

he could smell the acrid smoke. There was a small fire blazing under the horse trailer! A blown out tire on the furthest rear axle of the long trailer had caught fire from the friction of being dragged along the highway. Frantic with fear that the whole trailer would go up in flames, Joe grabbed the fire extinguisher he kept behind the truck's seat and dashed to the rear of the trailer to extinguish the fire. A good Samaritan pulled his pickup over to assist and with two men spraying the burning tire with retardants, the fire was soon out.

Joe said he was scared out of his mind to think what would have happened to his cargo of horses if PC had not insisted through her loud howling that he pull off the highway. As it was, Joe ended up with a damaged tire that he quickly replaced with a spare and a large patch of scorched paint on the under side of the trailer. When Joe got through with the tire change and was back in the cab, he gave PC a big cowboy kiss right smack between the ears. PC was once again content and Joe said she had no desire to exit the truck cab.

I guess heroes can come in small, purring packages, for Pole Cat possessed a sixth sense that animals can exhibit when danger is imminent. Without her insistent warning to Joe, my six horses and Joe's three might never had made it to Atlantic City Race Track. How do you thank a cat for that kind of service? I don't know, but for fifteen more years after this incident I had the best darn faithful stable cat in the country stationed at my stables.

Hope for Humphrey

By Noelle Hanek

There was only sixty minutes to go. The time was ticking down. This was how long Humphrey had before his short and brutal life would come to an end. So far, he spent most of his life living on the streets in Staten Island, New York. And now, he was in a cage on death row at a shelter in New York City. A volunteer who cared for Humphrey over the last few days, was starting to lose hope since he was now down to his very last hour.

Suddenly, a lady walked into the city shelter to donate food. The volunteer immediately started talking about Humphrey and asked the woman if she would take him. When she saw Humphrey's sweet face, she knew she could not just let him go. Since she fostered cats, she agreed to add him to her pride until he found his forever home. With only minutes to spare, Humphrey was whisked out of there and found himself with a group of cats and dogs who were ready for a new start.

I walked into the kitchen to prepare dinner for my cats, Furgus and Wilson, when I saw my mom's cell phone on the counter. A picture of a buff and white cat with the most precious face caught my eye. My mom was looking at an adoption website! Before I could ask her if she was looking at another cat, she scooped up her phone and walked into the other room. "Don't look at my phone!" she demanded. I thought it was strange, but I gave it little thought.

Soon after, my parents were spending a day in New York, or so I thought. As I was strolling through the house looking for something, I noticed that one of the cat carriers was missing. Things were getting clearer to me. My parents were not just spending time in New York, they were up to some cat business!

Later that night, I heard the car drive up the driveway. My heart pounded with excitement. My parents called me downstairs and said that they had a new family member to introduce to me. "Meet Humphrey!" they said as they proudly placed a thin, buff and white cat down in front of me and my brother Logan. Sure enough, it was the same cat I saw pictured on my mother's phone.

Humphrey tentatively approached me with his head down and I could tell he was very scared. Suddenly, he climbed under a recliner. When I bent down to find him, he was out of sight! As I looked closer, I noticed a hole in the underside of the chair that allowed him to climb straight up inside of it. In an attempt to coax him out of his hiding place, I would visit several times a day and leave food by his recliner to earn his trust. My patience paid off because one day he crawled out of his hiding spot, approached me, and to my delight, rubbed against me and gave a head butt. Day by day, Humphrey grew less tense around everyone, and seemed to come around more. I could see that he was finally getting to the point where he could call this place home.

But of course, life does not always work out that perfectly. There are twists and turns, bumps and falls. Humphrey developed a nasty rash on his face which turned out to be ringworm and a horrible cold. Since he never had the proper care that he deserved, we were not surprised when he became sick. Thankfully, he overcame his cold and over the next six weeks, my parents religiously applied his ringworm treatment until it finally cleared up.

Every cat has something special about them, but Humphrey is extremely unique. He thinks he's a dog or just aspires to be like one. Instead of purring to show his devotion, he head butts and squeaks instead. When he asks for attention, he yips like a dog. He also has an unlimited amount of energy and loves to play. Whenever we holler his name, he obediently comes running. Also, while my other cats are terribly fearful of dogs, Humphrey is the opposite. When he is at the vet and hears dogs barking, he runs to the edge of his carrier to get a better look. His foster mom also noted that he preferred the company of her dog to most of the cats.

Above all, Humphrey is the happiest creature I ever met and enjoys every minute of his life. I often think of that kind woman who rescued him from death row even though she already had a house full of cats and dogs. Her selfless act not only saved a cat, but it made our lives better too. I urge anyone interested in getting a cat to adopt because the benefits are endless. By giving a cat the loving life they deserve, you become a hero to that cat, make room for another cat at a shelter, and become the richest person in the world.

The Day I Met My Best Friend

By Noelle Hanek

After a long day, I threw my bookbag in the corner and I sat down. Next to me was my big orange and white cat who was simply content to be lying on the floor next to me. He was purring like a motor boat, looking up at me with his sweet large eyes. "Oh, where would I be without you?" I thought. My mind drifted as it often did, to the day my family adopted the cat who would be my best friend.

Four years ago, I was in the 3rd grade. Let me tell you, it had not been a great year for me. I lost all my "friends," disliked the school year, and suffered from anxiety. It was a lonely time. But there was someone else who was lonely as well. A big tomcat cat was out on the streets during the coldest days of the winter, begging for food and warmth. He was stranded by a donut shop near the parkway in New Jersey and was half frozen. When he spotted a police officer coming out of the shop, he darted over and rubbed against his leg begging for mercy. Thankfully, the officer worked with the local shelter and took pity on him. The officer opened the door to his car and let the frozen, sad looking cat climb into his warm car.

Two weeks later, I walked into the kitchen and found my Mother smiling at a picture she was holding. "Noelle," she said. "We are going to look at this cat today." She handed me a photo of a beautiful orange and white cat staring at the camera longingly. Although he was only a one-year-old cat, he looked much older and sophisticated since he had a goatee. "He looks just like Rusty, the cat I had as a child. I just have a good feeling about him," my Dad explained. As all these words were thrown at me I was in a state of complete shock and excitement. Although I had wanted a cat for so long, there was not any warning before today that my parents were considering it.

The shelter was about an hour away but my mother and I planned on making the trip. As we drove, I was thinking of how excited I was to meet him. Suddenly, a loud tinkering noise came from the back of the car. My mother was concerned the car was going to break down. "Maybe we should turn back?" she said as she questioned her decision to continue. I was determined to meet that sweet cat and nothing was going to stop us. I held the cross around my neck and quietly said prayers as my mother continued on. Soon after, the noise mysteriously stopped and we got closer to our destination. As we pulled into the shelter parking lot, I thought, "My cat is in there!"

On the door of the shelter, there was a poster advertising that the $25 adoption day was today. When my mother saw the sign, her face changed and she expressed concern that the kitty we had our hearts set on may already be gone. She picked up her pace and began speed-walking to the door. Surprisingly, when we got there, no one was around except a volunteer and she was standing by the door as if she had been waiting for us all morning!

After leading us down a dark hallway to a back room, she opened the door and led us to a corner cage where our orange and white cat was sitting. He stared back at me with worried eyes and I knew at once that he had been through a lot. Without wasting a second, the woman lifted him out of the cage and handed him to my mother. He spent little time in my mother's arms. Instead, he squirmed away with wide eyes and hid in a tube on the floor. My mother immediately began scanning the other cages with her eyes and asking to hold other cats but I already knew that this orange & white sweetheart was meant to be mine. I bribed him out of the tube with a toy and tried to make him feel more comfortable. Luckily, my mother picked up on my confidence in him and turned her attention away from the other cats. "This is the one for me." I told her and that was all she needed to hear. We filled out the paperwork and planned to take him home the next day.

When my mother went to adopt the cat we named "Furgus," the police officer who found him was there. After chatting with him, my mother discovered that the officer grew up in our town. He was just as surprised as we were to learn that the cat that he saved on the coldest day of the year was going to his hometown. "It's serendipity!" the officer declared.

Years have passed since that wonderful day when I found my best friend. Furgus and I are inseparable. He waits for me while I am at school and when I get home I am as happy to see him as he is me. When I am sick, he lies next to me and watches over me until I get better. When I am down he somehow always seems to know that I need extra attention. While I have made other friends since those gloomy times back in the third grade, there is no friend that can ever be better than my big orange and white tomcat.

About the Editor

A lifelong animal lover, Loren Spiotta-DiMare has been writing adult and children's books about her favorite subjects for over 40 years. She lives in rural Northwestern New Jersey with her husband, Lou, several dogs, four rabbits, numerous pet birds, and a Koi pond.

Over the course of her career, Loren has had many books published and numerous feature articles in regional and national magazines. Recognized by the Dog Writers Association of America, Humane Society of the United States, Doris Day Animal Foundation, USA Book News and New Jersey Press Women, Loren's work has been published both nationally and internationally.

In 2004, Loren added publisher to her list of credits by creating J. Pace Publications.

For more information about her books visit:
www.LorensReadingRoom.com

J. Pace Publications
PO BOX 301 • CALIFON • NJ 07830

HeinNouwens, ElenaShow, Cammep, Chipmunk131, Iaschi/MMH/Shutterstock.com

Made in the USA
Middletown, DE
30 October 2021

51098236R00096